Stories of New Hampshire

To Emilie

from

Brad

January 1, 1596

" there will never be
another one "

Walking through Crawford Notch, about 1850

Stories of New Hampshire

Eva A. Speare

New Hampshire Publishing Company
In Collaboration With the
New Hampshire Federation of Women's Clubs

ISBN: 0-912274-65-4
Library of Congress Catalog Card Number: 75-24515

New Hampshire Publishing Company, Somersworth 03878

Printed in the United States of America.

First Printing, hard bound edition: 1975
Second Printing, soft bound edition: 1977

Eva A. Speare: 1875-1972

Contents

Illustrations

The illustrations on pp. 20, 44, 78, 110, 166, and 222 are published with the permission of the New Hampshire Historical Society. The frontispiece, an engraving by Harry Fenn, is from *Picturesque America* published in 1872. The map on p. xx was taken from the original in the British Museum. The drawing on p. 192 is from *Scenery of the White Mountains* by William Oakes.

Foreword

The New Hampshire Federation of Women's Clubs, as its contribution to the State of New Hampshire's celebration of our nation's Bicentennial, has come up with a unique project, namely the publication of this volume of the late Mrs. Eva Speare's columns which deal with the history of New Hampshire.

The publication of this book seems particularly appropriate. Not only was Mrs. Speare for many years a leading member of the New Hampshire Federation of Women's Clubs, but she devoted much of her life to emphasizing the value of the history of the Granite State. She wanted always to keep clear the memory of the great men and women who by their effort and also through their sacrifices—often of their very lives—gave us New Hampshire as it is today. Eva Speare did not want us to take for granted the efforts of those who had come before.

When she was over ninety years old, Eva Speare became probably the oldest newspaper columnist in the nation. Once a week she honored our newspaper by writing a column. In spite of her own protestations that she was not a trained writer, it is my belief that she was sincerely pleased and happy by the fact that an amazing number of our readers expressed their gratitude and appreciation of those columns of hers. The simplicity and yet the strength and sincerity of her writing seemed to appeal to readers in New Hampshire of every age bracket and educational and economic background.

In the fullness of her years, when many an individual of similar age would have difficulty relating to the present, Eva Speare had an ability not only to be very much a part of the present, but also to bring the past into the present day, so that the two almost merged together to make life richer and more understandable for us all.

My only regret, entirely aside from my personal fondness for Eva Speare, was that she did not live to see her column published in our paper on her one-hundredth birthday.

And yet Eva Speare certainly does live through the columns in this book, which through the efforts of the New Hampshire Federation of Women's Clubs has been so appropriately published in this Bicentennial year. If Eva Speare were alive, nothing would please her more than this volume, dedicated to the Bicentennial of the nation she loved so well.

William Loeb, *Publisher*
Manchester Union Leader

Manchester, New Hampshire
July, 1975

Introduction

On February 28, 1970, the *Manchester Union Leader* began to publish a series called "Stories of New Hampshire." The column soon earned a wide and enthusiastic following. Every Saturday morning for almost two years, these delightful tales were required reading in thousands of New Hampshire homes. Even the publisher, whose idea it had been to recruit Eva Speare as a contributor, was surprised by the success of his experiment. "Mrs. Speare's column soon turned out to be one of the best features this paper had," William Loeb recalled in 1972. '"She had that hard-to-describe touch with her pen which made what she had to say and write extremely attractive. This newspaper was amazed by the different types of people, young and old and in various walks of life, who wrote to tell of finding her column so attractive."

When she wrote that first column, Eva was ninety-four years old. She died January 5, 1972, at the age of ninety-six. And although she began her newspaper career at what might justifiably be called an advanced age, she had certainly proved herself to be a professional. She did not miss a single publication date—ninety-seven in all, one for each year of her life plus one for the new year she was beginning.

"Eva Speare," wrote her publisher in his final tribute, "was one of the most remarkable individuals New Hampshire or any other state has produced in many a long year."

✿   ✿   ✿   ✿

She was born October 3, 1875, the daughter of George

and Mary Clough. Hers was a thoroughly New England up-
bringing; her father was a minister in Lawrence, Massachusetts, and Eva went to Vermont for her education as a teacher. She was graduated from Vermont Academy in 1896. Sev-
en years later she married Guy Speare, himself an educator.
The young couple lived in Littleton, where Eva joined the
local women's club. This was her first association with the
New Hampshire Federation of Women's Clubs—an association that was to last for almost seventy years.

In 1906 Mrs. Speare was employed as a teacher at Vermont's Bradford Academy, where to her delight she found a
telescope in good working order. Among her other contributions she soon became Bradford's astronomer-in-residence.
Years later, in one of her columns for the *Union Leader*, she
described how she alerted the town to the appearance of
Halley's Comet:

"My senior students and I were up early, sitting on the
board fence, waiting for the comet. Not knowing how the
comet would appear, I looked for it to rise in a vertical position. We were looking at Moosilauke Mountain. Suddenly,
parallel to the horizon lifted the glowing monster, spreading
the entire length of the mountain. Its ball of fire blazed larger than the full moon. The sparkling tail appeared to extend
about seventy feet along the summit of the mountain. The
comet moved with great rapidity, higher and higher along
the horizon. The students and I ran from home to home to
awaken folks whom we had promised to call. Soon the
small village was out in the morning air watching the comet
disappear over the northern horizon."

Such teachers are a priceless asset to the community that
is fortunate enough to employ them, and a few Bradford
Academy graduates may still remember the enthusiasm and
dedication of the young matron who awakened them to the
wonders of the sky.

After eleven years, however, Eva left the teaching profession to nurse her invalid mother-in-law. She then began a
new career as her husband's secretary, thoroughly enjoying
the revolution that came to education in those opening de-
cades of the twentieth century. She also undertook a variety

of public-service tasks—trustee of the Laconia State School for thirty-one years, member of state and local service boards in both world wars, fund-raiser for the Sceva Speare Memorial Hospital in Plymouth, and a leader of the drive to restore Fort Number Four in Charlestown.

Among her most satisfying tasks was her association with the New Hampshire Federation of Women's Clubs. Eva joined the Pemigewasset Women's Club in 1921, when her husband was superintendent of schools in Plymouth. She filled a number of offices in the organization and eventually became its president. In 1925 she was elected president of the New Hampshire Federation, and two years later she became president of the New England Conference of State Federations of Women's Clubs.

Among the other organizations she served with distinction were the Daughters of the American Revolution, the Daughters of the Founders and Patriots of America, the Daughters of Colonial Wars, and the Dames of the Court of Honor. Not surprisingly, Eva became a devoted student of colonial history, and more particularly the history of her adopted state of New Hampshire.

In 1932 she edited a volume entitled *New Hampshire Folk Tales,* published at her own expense by the Courier Printing Company of Littleton. It became a quiet best-seller, going through three printings in the year of publication, a fourth in 1933, and a fifth in 1945, before a revised edition was published in 1964. It was the proceeds from this book that helped launch the 1966 fund drive to restore "Old Number Four." Eva contributed $1,600 in royalties to begin the campaign. She directed the campaign herself, despite the fact that she had already celebrated her ninetieth birthday.

Among the books that flowed from her pen, as editor or author, were works about New Hampshire's historic bells, its colonial meetinghouses, its Indian tribes, and its seacoast region. She also compiled and published two genealogies and a history of her own family, the descendants of John Clough of Salisbury, Massachusetts; for eighteen years she edited a Clough family bulletin.

When Eva Speare died in 1972, an editorial by Reginald Colby of the Littleton *Courier* graciously summarized her contributions to the state:

"Now that she has finished the earthly tasks that kept her such a busy and useful citizen for so many years, it is fitting to recall some of the qualities . . . that still live on with her writings, in the memories of those who knew New Hampshire's 'unforgettable character.' Mrs. Speare had an honest commitment to preserve the best of the past and to strive to improve the present. She was an independent thinker and a persuasive speaker. She was industrious, loyal, and patriotic.

"She lived a courageous life. There was always something ahead of her to be done, even with failing eyesight. Although a gentle lady, she lived life with zest, but in moderation. She conserved her strength, not to reach the ripe old age of 96 but to live long enough to complete the rich legacy she left behind her."

✿   ✿   ✿   ✿

It was Eva's fondest wish that her "Stories of New Hampshire" would someday be published in book form, for the pleasure of residents and visitors alike, but more especially for the benefit of New Hampshire's younger citizens. A hard worker herself, even at an age when most people have long since retired to the sidelines, she believed that school children should have the opportunity to learn about the sacrifices made by the men and women who pioneered the Granite State.

The New Hampshire Federation of Women's Clubs is proud of its part in bringing Eva's dream to fruition. On behalf of the organization, I must express my gratitude to William Loeb and the *Union Leader*, who conceived and first printed these "Stories of New Hampshire."

Mrs. Glenn W. (Joy) Bricker, *President*
New Hampshire Federation of Women's Clubs

July 10, 1975

Stories of New Hampshire

Map of the New Hampshire settlements, mid-seventeenth century

{1}

Venturing
to the New World

THE INTREPID LIEF ERICKSON

Many years ago a minister was claiming that the first settlers of Portsmouth were Puritans when a voice from the
rear of the room interrupted: "Tut, tut, mon: the first settlers were English fishermen." The speaker was correct. To
explain how this came about is a long story.

It begins a thousand years ago when the northern countries of Europe were ruled by the Northmen who were invading the nations to the south. Along the North Atlantic
Coast a harbor was called a *vik*. The Northmen who lived
near the *viks* were called Vikings.

The vigorous Vikings were bold seamen who rode over
the ocean in their broad-beamed ships, open to the weather,
and propelled by one large square sail and sixteen or more
pair of oars in the hands of strong-armed oarsmen.

The Vikings discovered Iceland and inhabited the island
in the section where many hot springs cause the climate to
be more or less warm.

This story about Lief Erikson begins in Norway where
Lief's grandfather, named Thorwald, belonged to a family
of the nobility. The Vikings were fighting men who often
settled their quarrels in hand-to-hand combats. If a man
killed his foe, the law compelled him to banishment from
the country for a period of three years.

Thorwald killed a man in a contest. He fled to Iceland
with his family which included a son, born about 950 A.D.,
named Erik the Red, because of the color of his hair. Erik
grew to manhood in Iceland, married, and was the father of
three sons: Lief, Thorstein, and Thorwald.

While Erik was away from his home, an enemy killed
two of his slaves. In a fight for revenge, Erik killed five

men. He fled to a nearby island but his enemies followed him. A relative told him about the land to the north. He gathered a small crew of sailors for a voyage to these distant islands.

After sailing many days, a point of land was discovered that was covered with grass and a few trees. Erik named the point Greenland.

At the end of his three years of banishment, Erik returned to Iceland to tell about this new country where cattle could be raised. Soon a colony of families filled fourteen ships that landed in Greenland.

Erik's eldest son Lief grew to manhood in Greenland. He became a sailor and learned navigation, meaning that he studied the movement of the stars that guided him on the sea as the captain of a ship does today.

A cousin of Lief was a trader who owned a ship that was driven by a tempest over the ocean to the west where he saw a coast that was covered by trees. He did not dare to land there because reefs prevented it. The wind changed and he returned safely to Greenland.

When Lief heard about this voyage, he bought the ship from his cousin and, with a crew of thirty men, sailed to the west. He saw icy coasts, then wooded lands, and finally he discovered a safe harbor where the climate was warm.

The men erected a log cabin and remained there about a year. One day a sailor, who had lived in Germany and knew what he found, came bringing grapes. Then Lief named his new country Vinland. Lief noticed that the days were longer than in Greenland which indicates that Vinland might have been in Massachusetts.

In the spring the ship was loaded with lumber, because few trees grew in Greenland, and sailed for home. On the voyage fifteen shipwrecked people were rescued from an island. Because of this good deed and his discovery of a new country, Lief was given the title of Lief the Lucky.

Lief Erickson was the discoverer of some spot in New England in 1004 A.D. He died in Greenland in 1021 A.D.

THE VIKINGS IN NEW ENGLAND

The news that Lief the Lucky had discovered Vinland across the North Atlantic Ocean was heard soon in Iceland and Norway. This is proved by a round, stone tower that may be seen today at Newport, Rhode Island. The English settlers arrived there in 1639 and were astonished when they saw this well-constructed tower on a hill with a clear view of the harbor.

The tribe of Narragansett Indians did not remember about its origin. English architects declared that this tower was constructed in the same design as the towers in Norway before 1200 A.D.

There is an alphabet called runes that was used in Norway about 800 A.D., so long ago that its meaning was forgotten. Within this century scholars have discovered how to read this ancient alphabet.

Poems that were written in this runic alphabet about 1300 A.D., called sagas, have been translated today. One of them tells about Erik the Red and his son, Lief the Lucky.

In 1946 two scholars discovered five runes that were cut into a stone inside the wall of the round tower about fourteen feet above its base. These runes read, "ON, 1010 A.D." Because the windows in the tower face the harbor, it is believed that this tower was a lighthouse.

When the first English settlers arrived at Hampton, New Hampshire, 300 years ago, one family discovered a boulder upon their land with strange, white lines upon its surface. In 1902 a judge who was a descendant of this family, wrote an article for a newspaper in Philadelphia, Pennsylvania, that told about this boulder and the lines upon it.

This article attracted the notice of the Smithsonian Institution in Washington, D.C. Mr. Malcolm D. Pearson sent a picture of this boulder to a runologist, Mr. Ola Strandwold in Washington.

Mr. Strandwold interpreted the white lines to read, "Bui raised stone. 1043 A.D." He explained that Bui was the name of a famous family of navigators in Norway at that time.

This boulder may be found in Hampton about one-third of a mile from the Great Boar's Head. Along the Winnacunnet Road look on the right side for a gateway that is marked Surfside Park. Turn right from the gate into Thorwald Avenue and soon turn left into Emerald Avenue and on a lawn between two cottages the boulder stands.

Before his death, Mr. Strandwold visited Hampton and verified his translation. He wrote several books about the Norse boulders that are found along the Atlantic coast from Nova Scotia to Virginia that may be read among the collection in the Baker Library at Dartmouth College.

About thirty boulders with their runic inscriptions may be found in Massachusetts and Rhode Island where Vinland is supposed to have been settled by Lief the Lucky and later Vikings. Others are along the shore in Maine.

At the northern cape in Newfoundland the ruins of the foundations of stone buildings have been excavated and records of this village exist in Norway. Thus the proof that Vikings discovered New England about one thousand years ago is verified today.

The importance of this ancient history to New Hampshire is that these navigators drew maps of the coastline and made charts of their voyages that were preserved in Iceland.

CHRISTOPHER COLUMBUS

During the fourteenth century the Vikings lost interest in Vinland. Meanwhile merchants in Europe were beginning to desire to trade with Japan and India where Marco Polo and other travelers had visited across the miles by land. New designs for ships developed deeper hulls and two or more masts with divided sails. Seamen were venturing along the coast of Africa and into the Atlantic Ocean where they discovered the Canary Islands.

Venturing was the correct word. The earth was supposed

to be a land surface surrounded by water. If a ship should sail to the limit of the water, it would fall into space.

A boy was born in Genoa, Italy, about 1436 who was to change history. Christopher Columbus was the son of a weaver. He lived at a busy seaport where ships were constantly entering and leaving the harbor. It is not surprising that this lad became a sailor and in manhood he was a navigator. As he guided his ship on many voyages, he began to believe that the world was a ball rather than flat.

When he was forty years of age he heard about the Vikings and in 1477 he visited Iceland where he saw the maps that the Vikings drew of the coast across the sea. He studied their charts for navigation and became convinced that the world was round. He would sail west and find India and Japan.

Columbus was a penniless sea captain. He appealed to the king of Italy for ships without success. Portuguese ships were seeking for a route to the east. King Ferdinand of Portugal was not interested in sailing west. Columbus sent his brother to appeal to King Henry VII of England without results. Then Spain won a war against the Moslems and came into prominence. King Ferdinand paid little attention but Queen Isabella listened.

The queen promised to sell her jewels, if necessary, to provide ships. Merchants of Palos, Spain, furnished three ships: the *Santa Maria,* the *Pinta,* and the *Nina.* The *Santa Maria* was a modern, decked vessel but the other two were small boats known as "following ships."

On August 3, 1492, Columbus set sail from Palos, accompanied by eighty-eight men, heading south to the Canary Islands, and then across an unknown ocean. After two months without sighting land, the crew became frightened. They begged Columbus to turn back and even planned to imprison him and take control of the ships. Columbus was so certain that land would be discovered that he persuaded the sailors to continue a few more days.

Then they saw birds flying, next a poll that had been shaped by tools and a branch with strange red berries. At

ten o'clock on October 11 a sailor on the *Pinta* shouted
"Land." He saw light ahead. Soon the entire crew was cry-
ing "Land."

On the morning of October 12, 1492, Columbus, dressed
in his colored garments, went ashore expecting to meet people of India about whom Marco Polo had written. He saw
savages who thought his ships were strange birds. He found
a small island that was named San Salvador in the Bahamas.

Soon the ships embarked for Spain with gold, cotton,
strange birds and animals, and two natives to prove that
land was actually discovered. The return to Spain was excit-
ing. Soon a fleet of seventeen vessels and fifteen thousand
men were sailing for the discovery.

Columbus made three more voyages and on the fourth he
arrived at the coast of North America, yet he died without
knowing that he had discovered a new continent.

Although he never saw India, Columbus fastened the
name Indians upon the natives whom he found in the New
World.

Of importance to these stories about New Hampshire is
the fact that Columbus visited Iceland and learned about
the Vikings and their discoveries. Had he not studied their
maps he might have remained a sea captain and never a discoverer.

ENGLISH FISHERMEN
FIND THE SHOALS

When King Henry VII learned about the discovery by
Columbus, he employed a navigator, John Cabot, a native
of Genoa, Italy, who was living in London in 1497, to find
land for England.

John Cabot followed the route of the Vikings, sailing
southwest from England on May 2, 1497. Six weeks later he
saw the icy coast of Labrador on a day in June. Continuing
south, he is supposed to have landed upon the coast of

Nova Scotia where he unfurled the flag of England and proclaimed that he was taking possession of this land for King Henry VII.

On his return to England, he told King Henry that when he raised a weighted bucket from the sea, it contained fish. Then he cast a net and caught many fish. This was good news, because the population of England was increasing faster than the food supply.

Businessmen in England organized "guilds." The Fishmongers Guild was buying fish in Iceland. Now they would send their fleets of schooners to Nova Scotia. A fleet usually consisted of six ships, manned by a crew of sailors and about twenty fishermen.

With no power except the wind, the voyage from England to the fishing grounds required ten to twelve weeks. Early in the spring the fleets sailed from England. After a few years, each fleet had found its favorite bay or island for its annual landing.

The first necessity was salt to preserve the fish. Shallow vats were filled with seawater and exposed to the sunlight until the water evaporated—leaving a layer of salt in the vat.

Meanwhile limbs of trees that lined the shores were cut to make frames called "fish flakes" that were used during the summer to hang the salted, split fish to cure in the sun. Usually five schooners were fishing while the crew of one remained on shore to dry the fish. In September the hold of the ship contained a cargo of dry fish and the fleet arrived in England in November with a food supply for sale.

Today, fishermen know about a ledge, about 150 miles wide, that extends along the east coast of North America from Labrador to Carolina. The sea is 150 feet above this ledge, known as the Continental Shelf, and millions of many varieties of edible fish are swimming in these waters, sometimes called "the Grand Banks."

At some unknown date a fleet sailed farther south and discovered the Isles of Shoals with excellent fishing. After a few years, some of the fishermen decided to remain the entire year at the Shoals. They agreed upon a code of rules, one of them that no women should be allowed upon the islands.

When two fishermen brought their wives, the men decided that women were welcome, yet they added a rule that the woman must not sell intoxicating drinks. When the king of England discovered about this fishing village, he demanded taxes. The fishermen refused, saying they discovered these Isles, and the king did not possess them. Traditions tell that no taxes were ever paid while this village existed.

When we think of England in 1497, we must remember that the nation consisted of the small island off the coast of Europe. John Cabot's discovery was of historical importance.

Explorers began to visit our coast and make maps, because they hoped to discover a route through the continent to the Pacific Ocean. Martin Pring discovered the Piscataqua River in 1603. He reported that his dogs frightened the Indians far more than the roar of his guns.

Next came a Frenchman, Samuel de Champlain, who visited Rye Harbor in 1605. He continued north to the St. Lawrence River and up its stream to Lake Champlain. He claimed this territory for France and Quebec was settled in 1612.

A later king, James I, divided the coast of North America between two groups of nobles and merchants. The first, known as the London Company, received the region of Virginia and the Plymouth Company received what is New England today.

A settlement was made at Jamestown in Virginia in 1607 where Captain John Smith's story with Pocahontas became famous.

In 1614, John Smith was sent to America to search for gold and whales. He looked for land and found the Isles of Shoals that he named Smith's Isles. When he displayed a map of the region to Prince Charles, the name New England was proposed and so this title is ours today.

PANNAWAY

Before beginning the story about the first settlements in New Hampshire, it may be wise to attempt a picture, in the mind's eye, of the dense primeval forest that covered the region.

Primitive Abanaki Indians owned these woodlands where wild animals roamed beneath the trees.

After 1497 English fishermen sailed for more than one hundred years, back and forth from England, yet none of them ventured to live along the coast with the exception of the men on the Isles of Shoals.

About 1600 wealthy English noblemen and merchants organized the London Company and the Plymouth Company with the intention of taking possession of the coast that King James I claimed. Spain was finding hoards of gold in the south.

The London Company sponsored Jamestown in Virginia in 1607. The Pilgrims unintentionally landed at Plymouth, Massachusetts, in 1620.

Two wealthy fishmongers (traders) in the Plymouth Company conceived the idea that they would pay wages to English fishermen who would live and fish the year round in New England.

Ferdinand Gorges and John Mason appealed to King James I for land. He gladly gave to them the coast between the Merrimack and Kennebec rivers and inland to their sources.

Gorges chose the Kennebec section and named it Maine. His settlers decided that the climate was too cold and returned to England.

Mason named his section, between the Merrimack and both banks of the Piscataqua River, New Hampshire, in honor of his birthplace in Hampshire, England. He planned wisely when he employed David Thompson, a fisherman who had previously found a safe site for a settlement.

A high, rocky point was washed on the east by the Atlantic Ocean and on the west by a deep bay that he named Little Harbor and in the nearby forest was a bubbling spring of clear water. He named the site Pannaway, now situated in the town of Rye, New Hampshire.

Under a contract with John Mason, David Thompson selected a dozen fishermen, filled the ship *Jonathan* of Plymouth with all necessary equipment and, with his wife and probably several other wives, landed at Little Harbor in the spring of 1623 in Pannaway.

With the flat rocks on the shore and the sand and blue clay for mortar, a large house was soon constructed, also a storehouse, fish flakes, and salt works.

Here were about twenty people alone in the forest, yet Pannaway was not forgotten. Within a few weeks, Miles Standish, accompanied by several Pilgrims, sailed into Little Harbor asking to buy food for his hungry Pilgrims. Probably he had called at the Isles of Shoals where he learned about Pannaway.

The fact should be remembered that David Thompson divided his food with the Pilgrims. Fortunately a second ship arrived bringing twenty fishermen and more food.

Next, two castaway men sought refuge. One who escaped capture by Indians near Plymouth; the other, cold and almost naked after wandering through the forest, told that he was banished by the Pilgrims because he disagreed with their religious beliefs. David Thompson welcomed both men.

A forester under the king arrived and remained a month. Then an official who held a higher office was received with the honors due to him. Lastly, a baby boy named John Thompson, became the first white child to be born in New Hampshire.

After three years, David Thompson fulfilled his contract and departed to an island near Nahant, Massachusetts, still known today as Thompson's Island.

Pannaway did not remain a permanent settlement, yet it prospered so that within ten years these fishermen constructed fifteen sailboats and dories.

Gradually the name Pannaway faded from the story about the seacoast. Its fishermen scattered to other settlements or died.

In 1660 the property was purchased by John Odiorne whose descendants occupied Odiorne's Point until recent years. Today the United States military has possession of the shoreline. Tourists are welcome to visit the old cemetery and drink from the water of the ancient spring.

DOVER POINT

Pannaway was not alone in New Hampshire in the spring of 1623.

A second ship, the *Providence* of Plymouth, sailed up the Piscataqua River to a point where two brothers had decided to build their home. The families of Edward and William Hilton and their sister's, with possibly several other families whose names have been forgotten, arrived from London in the employ of John Mason in 1623.

The location of the village was named Hilton's Point, now changed to Dover Point. Fish and waterfowl were plentiful. With the wages and supplies that John Mason provided, Hilton's Point remained permanent, although little is known of its story.

About 1639 a considerable number of families came from western England, "said to have been of good estates and of some account for religion," with a leader named Wiggin.

A new village grew between the Piscataqua and the Bellamy rivers. There a small meetinghouse was erected, the first to be dedicated to the worship of God in New Hampshire.

Among these new villagers were men who were skilled shipbuilders. Richard Waldron employed them in his shipyard where seaworthy fishing boats were constructed. When pirates threatened the harbor at the mouth of the Piscataqua River, a vessel called a frigate was built that carried cannon and a crew of fighting men.

Other men in this new village were brickmakers, needed for fireplaces and chimneys. Pits of blue clay were discovered on the point. This was dug and spread thinly to dry. The large lumps were broken by men and oxen treading over them while they dried in the sun.

Sufficient moisture was added to permit the clay to be packed into brick-sized molds to be dried in the sun. Then these were baked in a kiln with a wood fire that was fed every two hours to keep the kiln exceedingly hot for a week.

On Dover Point, waterfalls ran sawmills that manufactured barrels and clayboards, now called clapboards. At that time the houses for the common people of England were made with walls of grass mingled with plaster that were covered on the outside with clayboards.

Clayboards were in great demand in England where the forests were no longer growing. Every clayboard was strictly measured to be four feet long, three inches wide, a half inch in thickness at one side and tapered to one-fourth inch on the other side. Thousands were shipped to England to cover the cottages in the villages.

Barrels and hogsheads were sent to the islands of the West Indies to be filled with rum or molasses. To be certain the barrels would not leak, the curved staves were taken apart and, with hoops to hold them together, tied into a bundle to be set up again after they arrived at the West Indies.

Before tea and coffee were imported into New Hampshire, beer was the common beverage. A brewery and a tavern, where the beer was permitted to be sold under strict laws, were necessary. Near the meetinghouse stood the stocks and pillory and the whipping post to punish offenders of the laws. There were no jails in New Hampshire.

A large tract of land was cleared of trees for a cow-common and another for sheep. Two never-failing springs supplied the water for the village. Women and children carried buckets of water for household use.

From the river an abundance of lobsters, oysters, and clams were available for everybody. In fact, clams were so plentiful that they were fed to the hogs.

Within twenty years Dover developed into a prosperous town. Before the death of John Mason, his employees prepared lists of supplies that they desired to be brought to them on the next ship and "When my ship comes in" must have become a wistful expression that was frequently repeated.

STRAWBERY BANKE

Anticipating that he would gain more money from his fishing trade and furs and timber, but hopeful that gold would be discovered, John Mason prepared for a third settlement in New Hampshire in 1631.

Having learned that the Hilton families were contented at Dover, eighty men, women, and their children sailed from Plymouth, England, in the ship named *Pied* (spotted) *Cow* early in the spring, expecting to establish a settlement near the mouth of the Piscataqua River.

Think for the moment about the living conditions for the twenty or more children aboard a small ship 300 years ago. With only the wind to blow against the sails across about three thousand miles of ocean, the voyage required three months of looking at the Atlantic Ocean surrounding the *Pied Cow*. No room to play, for every inch of space not occupied by the passengers and crew was filled with supplies for the colony.

Most necessary were casks of drinking water and ale to satisfy eighty persons for three months. Food that did not spoil consisted of salted meat, barley flour, oat meal, dried beans, and most important, lemons to prevent a skin disease called scurvy.

One deck was divided into small cabins with tiers of bunks for sleeping. The women cooked the bean porridge and barley cakes over small stoves with charcoal fires. The lights were lanterns that used whale oil.

Amusement for children was difficult. At that time pencils and paper, storybooks, and toys were unknown. Probably the mothers told stories, invented games, and sang songs in the narrow aisles between the bunks.

The hull was filled with guns, powder, and bullets, plus many tools such as axes, saws, and hammers. Probably a number of cows were aboard. Humphrey Chadburn, an engineer, had packed the frame for a large house he would erect before the *Pied Cow* returned to England. Shelter was needed, because packs of fierce wolves and other wild animals roamed through the forest. Indians might be dangerous foes.

From Plymouth, the ship sailed south to the Azore Islands where fresh water was supplied, then west to Nova Scotia, and south along the coast of Maine until the captain found the mouth of the Piscataqua River.

Imagine the joy of finding ripe strawberries scattered through the grass. While these pioneers lived, the name of their town was Strawbery Banke. Here were eighty persons alone in a strange country, seeing only the sky, the river, and trees. One man was immediately appointed to drive away the wolves, doubtless by keeping a fire blazing day and night.

The "Great House" was erected for the home of these eighty pioneers. It stood on Court Street about where the Strawbery Banke Center is found today in Portsmouth. Next, Humphrey Chadburn built a number of sawmills, one at every waterfall that provided force enough to turn a waterwheel.

The Indians came into the village with their furs to sell. When they saw anything in town they liked, they took it. To them this was not stealing, because in their villages everything belonged to the tribe. For protection of the village, Chadburn built a stockade, meaning a high wall of logs that was set vertically into the ground. This log wall began at the bank of the river and extended to a ravine called the

Lower Mill Pond that filled and lowered twice a day when the tide rose and fell. Thus the village was protected from wolves and Indians.

In New Hampshire, guns were neither sold nor given to Indians. Unfortunately, the French in Canada were permitting friendly Indians to carry guns.

Suddenly John Mason died in 1635. He had invested so much of his wealth in his settlement that his widow was unable to pay the wages to the settlers. His estate was willed to two teen-aged nephews, one of whom soon died.

The greedy superintendents who represented John Mason in the three towns began to grasp for whatever they desired. One of them sold in Boston 300 yellow cattle that John Mason imported to New Hampshire and kept the price of the sale in his own pocket.

The heads of families called town meetings to frame laws to control their situation. This was the beginning of democracy in New Hampshire.

EXETER AND HAMPTON

Three years after the death of John Mason in 1635, a new town was developed by Puritans from Massachusetts. The Bay Colony of Massachusetts possessed a charter from the king of England that permitted the householders to own their land and homes and the right to vote in the General Assembly if they were members of the Puritan church.

The religious beliefs of the Puritans were strict. If a person disagreed with them he was banished from the colony. The Reverend John Wheelwright disagreed. With ten families who believed with him, he purchased thirty acres from the Swampscott tribe of Indians along the bank of the Swampscott River.

Although these Indians had no knowledge of reading, this clergyman thought that he was making legal arrangements when he gave to them a written agreement which the Indians did not understand and did not honor.

The new town, named Exeter, was the first in New Hampshire to be established for religious freedom. More objectors increased the population, some of whom were shipbuilders. Exeter became famous for its shipyards.

Evidently Exeter feared the Indians. The oldest house now standing in New Hampshire was erected by John Gilman for a garrison house, meaning a refuge for the inhabitants if attacked by Indians.

The second story projects several feet beyond the lower story with an open space in the floor that permits water to be poured below to extinguish a fire, or boiling water to repel Indians.

This town became prominent in military affairs of the colony and was the capital of the province and later of the state when its constitution was adopted.

South of Exeter a company of Puritans from Norfolk, England, was granted 100 square miles beyond the north bank of the Merrimack River in 1638 by the Massachusetts Bay Colony. This was the same land that King James I had given to John Mason,

With Reverend Srephem Bachiler (old spelling), their leader, fifty-six families desired freedom to worship God as they believed. They possessed considerable wealth and imported 100 cows with the intention of using the marshes along the coast to raise cattle. The town was called Winnacunnet, now Hampton.

Inland, beyond the coast, the village grew rapidly. Two-story houses were erected with oak framework so firmly fastened together, many of them are standing today. Their meetinghouse was surrounded by a stockade that enclosed sufficient space to protect the entire population from hostile Indians.

One of these families discovered the Norse Rock that is mentioned on page 5.

The small bay now called Rye Harbor was soon busy with boats that carried on trade along the coast which proves there were fishermen who knew the skill of building boats.

Hampton folk believed in witches. Goody Cole was accused of witchcraft in 1656. She was tried in court, convicted, and the town paid her board in the jail at Salem, Massachusetts. She was released to care for her sick husband but was jailed again after he died.

After the taxpayers grew tired of paying the annual tax for her board at Salem, she was again set free. She died in poverty, alone, and was considered a guilty woman.

The tradition is that she was buried by the roadside and small trees were driven into her grave to prevent her ghost from coming to the surface of the ground. Old ghost stories are many in Hampton. The religious Puritans suffered from superstitions long ago.

Within twenty years after 1623 the province of New Hampshire contained four settlements, separated by several miles of dense forests. The only communication between them was by sailing ships.

PAPISSECONEWA, SAGAMON.

Only known likeness of Chief Passaconaway of the Penacooks

{2}

The Massachusetts Connection

A UNION WITH MASSACHUSETTS

After the death of John Mason, Dover and Portsmouth were managed by the superintendents John Mason had appointed, without satisfaction to anyone.

Among the families were honest pioneers. Another element was rude sailors and fishermen who were often offenders against society. Stealing, fighting, and worse crimes were committed constantly.

A new plan for government was proposed by the four towns: Dover, Strawbery Banke, Exeter, and Hampton. The Massachusetts Bay Colony possessed a charter that permitted the heads of families to own their lands and homes. Also their courts were established to enforce laws that were enacted by their General Court.

New Hampshire requested union with Massachusetts in 1641. The Bay Colony sanctioned this appeal without demanding that the voters be members of the Puritan Church as was the rule in Massachusetts.

By this arrangement, the heads of families would own their land and homes, a right they believed they had earned when they cleared the fields of trees and stumps with only oxen to help them.

Each of the four towns elected two representatives who attended the General Court in Massachusetts to share in enacting laws.

Soon the nephew of John Mason came of age and demanded rent from every householder, only to be informed that they were a part of Massachusetts and did not owe him money. Thus a long quarrel began because New Hampshire landowners paid taxes to Massachusetts.

DARBY FIELD
CLIMBS MOUNT WASHINGTON

One of the early stories about New Hampshire describes the exploit of a settler of Dover in 1652. Darby Field was an Irishman who was blessed with a considerable gift of curiosity. While his remarkable adventure is not unknown, yet it bears repetition at this period among these tales.

Durham Point of the present day was covered with grass that attracted several families to build their homes across Great Bay from Dover Point. Darby Field was a fisherman who also ran a ferry from the Durham shore across to Fox Point. A small ravine in the rocky shoreline permitted him to draw his boat into its shelter not far from his buildings.

When he was fishing along the shore of the ocean, he looked at the northern horizon at two dark peaks that stood clearly alone, as one sees them today. Where were these lonely mountains and how far distant?

One morning early in June he decided to solve the puzzle. Evidently he collected whatever he considered necessary for an unknown trip of exploration, then sailed northward along the coast until he discovered a stream that flowed from the direction of these peaks. Up the Saco River he traveled, alone in the forest.

One imagines that he watched for a cliff on the bank of the stream where he could safely rest through the night, protected by a fire to discourage the wolves and other beasts. Probably he enjoyed a meal of fresh salmon or trout with perhaps corn bread.

He paddled on for several days until he arrived at a village of about two hundred Indians. No doubt he was the first white man many had ever seen. He managed to tell that he wished guides to the mountains. No Indian wished to join him because on the summits was the dwelling of Manitou, an evil spirit who would kill any man who ventured into his land of clouds.

With some gifts Darby Field persuaded two Indians to join him, although many walked as far as the climb began.

Safely the ascent was made up the east side of Mount Washington. They saw snow and at the summit a large lake in the valley below, which was a bank of white clouds. When the three walked safely back to the village, the Indians were astonished.

After thirteen days of absence from home, Darby Field arrived at his door. After satisfying his curiosity with such pleasure, he is reported to have repeated the journey the following year.

The first mention of the White Mountains in print occurs in John Josselyn's *New England's Rarities Discovered* printed in 1672: "It is to Darby Field of Piscataqua that the credit is now generally assigned of being the first explorer of the White Mountains."

PORTSMOUTH IN 1650

After twenty-seven years, the name Strawbery Banke lost its significance, especially for a group of later families, and a more dignified name of Portsmouth was adopted in 1650 in honor of the residence of John Mason in England.

The early families built homes in the vicinity of the present Court Street that became "the South End" while later arrivals lived further up the river at "the North End." The oldest house in Portsmouth stands today there on "the Christian Shore" as a rough sailor named it. Two Jackson brothers erected the two-story home in 1664 and the place is worthy of a carefully planned visit.

Other families removed to Great Island at the mouth of the harbor to escape the troublesome Indians. A small fort was constructed on the island and was armed with four cannon for protection from pirates. This village became Newcastle.

In 1656 a young immigrant to Massachusetts, named John Pickering, decided to live in Portsmouth to engage in the lumber business. He needed a sawmill but could not find a waterfall for power.

Although John Pickering never learned to write his name, in company with many other settlers, he displayed his mechanical ability when he applied to the townsmen to grant to him the right to construct a tidewater dam across the entrance to a small ravine that extended inland from the bank of the Piscataqua River and filled and fell with the tide. This inlet was called the Lower Mill Pond.

A meetinghouse had been built upon Meetinghouse Hill at the South End that obliged the families at the North End to walk around the Mill Pond to attend church on the Sabbath.

Permission was granted to John Pickering to build a tidewater dam if he would construct its width to provide a pathway along the top for a shorter walk to the meetinghouse on the Sabbath.

John Pickering closed the wide mouth of the ravine with a high and wide stone wall with a space at its center that was filled by a wooden gate that was gradually raised when the tide flowed up the river and lowered when it flowed out over the gate. This made a waterfall to run his sawmill. This idea for a tidewater dam was followed at several inlets along the coast to run gristmills.

The saws in these early mills moved up and down through a log that was no more than a foot in diameter. Larger logs were cut by pit saws wielded by muscular workmen. One man stood upon the log to guide the saw to keep the same thickness of the board from end to end. Down in the pit, another man pulled the saw down and pushed it back up through the log. The sawdust must have filled his eyes and hair.

When one visits colonial houses and admires the wide wainscoting and panels, remember that these were cut in pit saws by the muscles of our ancestors.

KING PHILIP'S WAR

The year 1675 saw the beginning of fifty years of savage warfare with Indians. The trouble was begun by King Philip as he was known to the English rather than by his Indian name. He was the son of Massasoit, the chief of the Wampanoag Tribe, who gave corn to the Pilgrims when they were starving in 1621.

Within twenty years from 1620, the colony of Massachusetts numbered 20,000 settlers. King Philip saw his forest hunting grounds disappearing. The deer and wild turkeys had been the food supply of his tribe and King Philip knew of no means to prevent their disappearance except to kill the white men.

He sent messengers to urge all of the tribes to unite with him—to the Saco tribe in Maine and the tribes in New Hampshire. The Indians along the coast of New Hampshire did not immediately agree with King Philip. An unfortunate incident changed their attitude.

The squaw of Squando, the leader of the Piscataqua tribe, was in a canoe on the river with her baby boy. A group of drunken sailors decided to test a rumor that an Indian baby would swim as naturally as a dog.

Approaching the canoe, a sailor snatched the baby and tossed him into the river. The squaw plunged into the water and rescued her child, but the sudden shock of the cold water caused the infant to sicken and die. Then Squando agreed that white men were not welcome and he influenced the tribes along the coast to unite with King Philip.

Without warning during the summer of 1674, the homes of families were attacked. The entire family was killed with Indian cruelty, the buildings burned, and cattle slaughtered. Fear spread through the four towns in New Hampshire. Fire, cruelty, and fear were weapons of Indians.

Preparations for defense were begun. Dover surrounded five houses with stockades of logs set upright into the ground and sharpened to a point at the top. Every person in the town was assigned to one of these houses for refuge whenever a warning of a raid of the Indians was signaled by a drum.

In Hampton a log wall enclosed sufficient space to accommodate the entire population of the village. Exeter protected the large garrison house that John Gilman had already built to receive the residents of that small village.

Portsmouth from its beginning had feared the Indians. The Great House was surrounded by a stockade. In King Philip's War a "picked wall" was extended from the bank of the river across the village to the Lower Mill Pond. This prevented a sudden attack against the homes in the lower village.

As soon as possible, guards were enlisted and supplied with guns and ammunition in both colonies. King Philip and his Wampanoag tribe lived in a well-protected location in Rhode Island known as The Great Swamp.

On December 12, 1675, the guards of Massachusetts destroyed this stronghold but King Philip escaped capture. He continued to lead his army of warriors until August 12, 1676. A group of scouts in Massachusetts surrounded his hiding place and shot him where he was sitting upon a log in the forest.

As soon as their leader was dead, the tribes lost courage and their attacks ceased, but not until ten villages in Massachusetts had been burned and hundreds of men, women, and children had been killed with horrible cruelty. The colony was in debt to the amount of £100,000. A pound was then worth about three dollars in modern money.

In New Hampshire many homes outside of the villages were destroyed and the families killed. The Penacook tribe refused to join in this war. Their leader, Wonalancet, obeyed the advice of his father, Passaconaway, which saved many lives.

SHIPBUILDING

Although English fishermen established the colony of New Hampshire in 1623, within the following twenty years shipbuilding became a rival industry.

With the exception of shelter and food, every necessity for human living was imported and soon the products of the forests were exported. An increasing number of ships were demanded.

Only skilled ship carpenters knew the shape of the deep, curved hull that could not capsize in a gale or fill with water and sink. The king and council refused certificates (passports) to experienced shipbuilders to permit them to leave England.

Yet, ship captains and fishermen acquired the knowledge to build seaworthy vessels. Such names in the colony as Richard Waldron in Dover, Edward Gilman in Exeter, Hercules Hunkins, John Hall, John Heard, and Hateevil (what a name to give to a baby boy) Nutter were well-known shipbuilders in the colony in 1640.

In the winter months, a ship would be constructed in the forest, then drawn by oxen to the ice of a river and launched by nature when the ice melted in the spring.

Masts that supported the sails in a strong wind without breaking were in greatest demand. The king appointed an officer with a large salary, known as the master of the king's woods to select masts for the king's navy. These trees were to be over 100 feet in height without lower branches growing from their trunks. These trees were marked by a "broad arrow," a design like a V cut deeply into the bark in a horizontal position. Woe to anyone who felled such a mast tree without authority from the master of the king's woods.

Only skilled lumbermen cut such mast trees. First the direction that the tree should fall was determined. Then every tree that was growing in this path was cut and a cushion of large branches covered the ground to break the fall of the giant tree.

A road was made to a stream and many yoke of oxen drew the mast to the stream to float it to a wharf where a mast-ship waited to transport it to England for the navy. Today in southern New Hampshire signs are found that mark old mast roads and mast yards.

Soon France and Holland were paying high prices in New Hampshire for masts. This displeased the king. A Navigation Law was enacted that masts should be sold only to

England. However, the ocean was wide and captains of ships were wise about sailing routes.

After years, the king became convinced that a ship was constructed at one-third less cost in New Hampshire where the timbers were growing. He granted passports to ship carpenters and permitted the vessels for the navy to be built in the colony.

Fortunes were accumulated by families who owned ship-yards. A ship would carry a cargo of bundles of materials for barrels and hogsheads that were assembled in Barbados in the West Indies and filled with rum or molasses for the same ship to carry to England. This cargo would be sold to merchants and often the ship was sold. Or another cargo of goods for the colony was sold when the ship returned to New Hampshire and would soon be ready for another voyage.

Several families continued with fishing and owned 100 or more schooners in their fishing fleets that produced hundreds of tons of salt fish for the markets in England.

Thanks to the primeval forest and to the fish in the sea and the hard work of the settlers, the colony of New Hampshire was well on its way to prosperity at the end of the first fifty years after John Mason paid fishermen to venture to live in an unknown land.

The name of John Mason, fishmonger, founder of the colony of New Hampshire, should be remembered with highest honor.

Within the New Hampshire Historical Society's collection is a price list by the king's agent or ship master. Thirty-four large masts were listed at £900 and thirty-three at £700; twenty-four yardarms at £320 and thirty-one bowsprits at £425. The prices varied with the diameter, which was from thirty-four to twenty-four inches for masts, twenty-four inches for yards and thirty-five inches for bowsprits, at their bases.

Belknap's history in the period after the American Revolution stated that a mast with a diameter of thirty-six inches was priced at £147.

SPORTS DAY AT DOVER

King Philip's War was a surprise to the colonies. The men in authority conferred about how to teach the Indians that such a war must never occur again. It was decided that if the chiefs of the tribes were punished, then the Indians would learn a severe lesson.

Major Waldron, the shipbuilder of Dover, was placed in command. He was expected to invite the Indians to a day of sports at Dover which the Indians were known to enjoy. This would call the chiefs of the tribes together in one place where they could be captured.

Fearing that the Indians might become suspicious if a town in the Bay Colony was selected, Dover seemed to be the place for this plot. Major Waldron objected to this trickery, but he was urged by many men who had suffered in the war and even by officials in England. Unfortunately, he finally approved the plan.

Four hundred Indians accepted the invitation to Dover and eagerly joined in the games. When everyone gathered closely in a crowded game, guns gave the signal. Hundreds of the Indians were captured.

The chiefs were taken to Boston where they were hung. Two hundred Indians were placed aboard ships, taken to England, and sold for slaves.

Evidently the English did not realize that Indians never forgot a kindness, and also always remembered an enemy. Time taught the truth of this Indian characteristic.

The Penacook tribe came to the sports day with their chief, Kancamagus, who was the grandson of the oldest son of Chief Passaconaway, who advised that his tribe should live in peace with the white man.

Wonalancet became chief of the Penacook tribe and followed the advice of his father. When Kancamagus became chief of the Penacooks, associated with him was a son of Wonalancet named Paugus, who was a foe of the English. While Kancamagus watched the trickery at Dover, his friendship changed. He became a bitter foe and encouraged the Penacook tribe to become secret enemies in New Hampshire.

THE NAVIGATION LAWS

The trouble with the Indians ceased for a while, but a new problem arose. The grandson of the nephew to whom John Mason willed his property demanded that families in New Hampshire pay rent to him or remove elsewhere.

He appealed to the king of England for assistance in collecting not only present rent but back payments also. The king agreed with this. John Tufton Mason appointed an official to collect the rents.

The heads of families refused this demand, declaring that they had been united with the colony of Massachusetts under its charter since 1641 and that this charter gave to them "the right of soil" where they had cut the forests, pulled out the stumps of trees, and dragged the boulders into stone walls to clear their farms.

The king declared New Hampshire a separate colony and a popular citizen of Portsmouth, named John Cutts, was appointed provincial executive, meaning governor. Laws and courts were established and an assembly, or legislature, was elected by seventy-one eligible voters of Portsmouth, sixty-one of Dover, fifty-one of Hampton, and twenty of Exeter. Thus, local self-government was introduced into the colony.

With the intention to prohibit trade with France and Holland, the king and his councilors began to restrict trade, except to England. All goods must be purchased in England and transported in English ships with a crew of English sailors.

Almost all articles could be bought for less in other countries. Now the prices were determined in England and duties were collected also. Another restriction was that all exports from the colonies must be sent to England, or English colonies such as the Barbadoes and other islands in the West Indies.

New Hampshire was producing the products of the saw-mills, furs, masts, and potash, which was the basis of gun powder. Naturally these navigation regulations were disliked in the colonies and evasion was encouraged by the officials in New Hampshire.

The thirteen colonies were carrying on a busy coastal trade in corn, fish, pork, and lumber. New England was buying tobacco and wheat from the South. Gossport on the Isles of Shoals numbered six hundred inhabitants.

Sea captains soon learned to fly the English flag when entering a harbor and officials ignored from whence the goods were shipped.

Note—this condition existed a century before the American Revolution.

THE ATTACK ON DOVER

Twelve years passed after the day of sports at Dover. Meanwhile the Indians were planning for revenge. They gradually established such friendly relations with the people at Dover that all hostility disappeared. The gates of the stockades were not locked at night and in cold periods lonely squaws were permitted to sleep before the fireplaces in the homes with no fear of danger from them.

One chilly evening in the spring of 1689 several squaws asked for shelter in a number of homes. When everyone seemed to be sleeping, the squaws opened the doors of the homes and the gates of the stockades to permit the attacking Indians to rush into the village.

Now armed with guns, the invaders attacked the houses of the leaders and killed these men and captured the young citizens. Small children were killed but all older youths and the women were gathered into three groups that were hurried into the surrounding forest with the intention of taking them to Canada to be sold for servants at Quebec and Montreal.

Several men escaped and ran to the other towns for help. Two of the groups of captives were rescued from the for-

est, but the third company was hurried by the water route
of lakes and rivers and were sold in Canada.

Richard Waldron was the victim for punishment. He was
cruelly tortured for hours before he died. After this attack,
peace never existed between white men and red men in
New England.

Hostilities increased when the French and English in Europe began the Hundred Years' War in 1690. The first of its
four sections was called King William's War that continued
until 1697.

The French in Canada made the Iroquois their allies by
gifts of guns and ammunition and sent them to attack the
English in New England. Portsmouth suffered raids by Iroquois from Maine where they had established villages in the
Kennebec Valley.

Portsmouth was in constant danger. A raid south of the
town killed many elderly people in an attack known to this
day as Brackett's Lane Massacre. Guards followed these Indians and overtook them while they were eating breakfast
at a place now called Breakfast Hill near Portsmouth, where
all of these Indians were surprised and killed.

Situated across Great Bay from Dover is Durham Point
where Darby Field built his home in 1640. Twelve families
had built garrison houses around the shore and upon higher
ground.

The Swampscott tribe, always more or less hostile, now
became dangerous foes. One morning they attacked and
burned five garrisons. When they approached a house, they
would promise no attack if the doors were quickly opened.
When the Indians were admitted, they killed the family and
burned the dwelling.

The home of Darby Field had been purchased by Thomas Bickford. He saw the smoke from other houses and sent
his family far out upon Great Bay in a canoe. Then he
opened his windows and, as the Indians came near, began
to shout orders while he appeared wearing a cap; then with
a hat, and later with some other head gear while he continued to shout orders. The Indians did not enter his garri-

son because they feared a group of gunners. Other garrisons on the higher ground were able to defend their houses before the Indians arrived.

In the town of Exeter, new garrisons were erected for protection. At the home of Stephen Dudley the women were boiling soft soap when the Indians attempted to burn the place. From the upper projection of the garrison, hot lye soap was poured upon the heads of the attacking Indians who fled screaming with pain.

The Indians tried various schemes to tempt the guards to open the doors of the garrisons. At one place the watch saw that the cows were in the nearby cornfield. Knowing that the fence around the field was too strong for the cows to break through it, Indians were suspected and no one ventured outside for several days. Later, when the pasture was searched the ambush that the Indians had prepared was discovered.

At another place hogs were kept and allowed to roam into the surrounding woods for acorns. Indians were feared when the hogs did not return for their evening feeding. In the nights grunts were heard, indicating that the hogs had come home. But the trick did not work—nobody went outside to take care of the hogs. The hogs never came home.

THE INDOMITABLE HANNAH DUSTIN

At the beginning of the history of New Hampshire women were important, yet few acquired fame. The first heroine in the state was Hannah Duston (the early spelling of the name), famous throughout the nation because she possessed courage to kill ten Indians to save her life.

Hannah was born in Haverhill, Massachusetts, on December 23, 1657, the daughter of Michael and Hannah (Webster) Emerson. Hannah Webster Emerson distinguished these names long before Daniel Webster and Ralph Waldo Emerson were born.

Haverhill was a forested area in 1635 when only a few

families were scattered in the south section of the present city. Michael Emerson built his home where Boardman Street is today, on the bank of Mill Brook that flows from Ayers Pond, now called Saltonstall Lake. There Hannah Emerson was born.

Sometime later the grantors of the town offered to Mr. Emerson a tract of land, now the corner of Summer and Winter streets, "if he would go further into the woods," which he accepted. There Hannah lived until she married Thomas Duston, December 3, 1677, at the time when King Philip was killing the English because they were destroying his hunting grounds and food supply.

Thomas Duston built his home on the bank of Sawmill Brook, called later Little River, in the vicinity of Eldora Street in the North Parish. He started the first brickyard in the town.

The couple had seven children and Hannah was recovering seven days after baby Martha was born when on the morning of March 15, 1697, Indians were approaching the home. Hannah urged Thomas to save the children. He told the seven to run into the woods toward the garrison house of Onesiphorus Marsh near the bank of the Merrimack River while he mounted his horse and fought the Indians.

Meanwhile the Indians killed the baby and captured Mrs. Duston and her nurse, Mrs. Mary Neff, and compelled them to leave the house that was pillaged immediately. The March wind must have been cold and the river at flood, yet it is believed that the Indians, with their captives, paddled up the stream to an island at Penacook, New Hampshire. The story is related that while in camp, Hannah cooked a soup that the Indians ate heartily, then they fell soundly asleep. It is believed that Hannah added the roots of a plant possessing soporific power.

While the Indians slept soundly, Hannah and a captive boy killed ten Indians with tomahawks, took their scalps, and then the three captives fled down the river in a canoe safely to Haverhill.

Thomas Duston was building a brick home a short distance from the original house and he had taken his children there. Hannah returned in safety to join them.

On the bank of the river at the mouth of Creek Brook is now a park. A large millstone marks the spot where they beached the canoe. On Broadway stands the house of George Corliss, erected in 1640, which was the home of Mrs. Mary Corliss Neff, to which she returned from captivity.

The family continued to live in the brick house many years. Mr. Duston died in 1732. Then Hannah lived with a son in another adjacent home. There she died in 1736. This home is marked by a large boulder.

In 1938 the brick garrison house to which Hannah returned was damaged by fire, but it has been restored by the Duston-Dustin Garrison Association which was organized in 1945.

Every visitor to Haverhill finds the Common, near Main Street, to view and photograph the statue of Hannah Dustin, the first monument to be erected in America in memory of a woman. On each of the four sides of its base is a bronze bas-relief depicting an event in her captivity. This statue was the gift of E.J.M. Hale and was erected November 25, 1879.

Also, a visit should be made to the large, brick mansion called "The Buttonwoods," because of the large knots or buttons that grow upon the trunks of the many surrounding sycamore trees.

Here in the museum of the Haverhill Historical Society, among the many relics of the Dustin family, may be seen a large square of white linen in which Hannah wrapped the ten scalps of the Indians to prove that she and Samuel Lennards, a teen-age boy, actually killed ten Indians.

At the island near Penacook where Hannah Dustin was held captive is another monument erected in her honor.

New Hampshire and Massachusetts share in this remarkable story that was courageously acted out in the spring of 1697.

THE LAST OF THE ABANAKIS

The second period of the Hundred Years' War between England and France began in 1703, known as Queen Anne's War. During the following fifteen years no colonist slept in safety.

Iroquois united with the Penacook tribe in vicious attacks. Up the coast into Nova Scotia the unsuccessful expedition to Port Royal was made and the story of Acadia furnished the poet Longfellow with his tale of *Evangeline*.

Because of a grudge against Pastor Williams, on a February night in 1704, the Iroquois burned half of Deerfield, Massachusetts, killed scores and captured 111 prisoners who were compelled to tramp through the snowdrifts while the Indians walked upon snowshoes. Frozen deer meat was their food and when one fell exhausted instant death followed. Mrs. Williams was left to freeze in the snow.

In the towns of New Hampshire families lived in garrison houses or near such a refuge. Within a circle of twenty-five miles around Dover, seven hundred persons were killed.

About 1712 the court in Massachusetts offered ten pounds for every scalp of an Indian and more if an "Indian nest" (meaning a village) was destroyed.

Among the prisoners from Deerfield was a lad of twelve years named Thomas Baker. He suffered cruelly for weeks until a Frenchman from Montreal paid the Iroquois for him. In Montreal he talked with a girl of his age named Christine Otis who told him about how her mother concealed her during the attack at Dover in 1689 and how they were taken to Canada by way of the present town of Plymouth where there was an Indian nest.

Thomas Baker and three companions managed to escape and returned to Deerfield in 1705 in a starving condition. Now twenty years of age, Baker enlisted thirty-four scouts and an Indian guide. They tramped up the Connecticut Valley, across the divide into the Merrimack Valley from Lake Tarlton to the village of the Indians. When he saw the young hunters leave the village, he immediately shot every

Indian that he found, old and young, burned their wigwams and fled southward. Meanwhile a small Indian boy was running to call the hunters.

Six miles from the burning village Baker was overtaken. Every scout took shelter behind a tree and killed many of the Indians. Baker and the Indian chief, Wattermunus, exchanged shots, but Baker was quicker on the trigger and killed the chief instantly. Only pausing to take his scalp, the scouts fled southward. Massachusetts paid ten pounds to Baker for this scalp.

Finally, the English are supposed to have caused a fatal epidemic among the Penacooks that reduced their warriors to 250 men. Then their bitter enemies, the Mohawk tribe, were informed of this situation. The Mohawks with overwhelming numbers attacked the Penacooks at their village near the present Concord.

The Penacooks fled to a secret refuge on an island in Lake Winnisquam which the Mohawks soon discovered. All day the Penacooks fought to their death. When darkness ended the fight, Kancamagus managed to escape with a remnant of his tribe in canoes across the lake to Mohawk Point, seen today from the bridge across Lake Winnisquam. Up the Winnipesauke River and by well-known trails, these Penacooks fled to the forests near Sandwich.

According to Indian custom, the Penacooks carried the bones of Chief Passaconaway with them and deposited them in a ravine upon the mountain that now bears his name. After recuperating a few weeks, Kancamagus led his Penacooks on into Canada. Paugus, the Penacook, survived the battle with the Mohawks at Lake Winnisquam. He joined the Pequakets and Ossipees, urging them to drive the English from the Saco River Valley.

When bands of English soldiers opposed them, the tribes vanished into the deep woods where they knew the forest trails. But they returned to raid villages, even into Maine at Casco and Kennebunk, where several hundred of the villagers were murdered.

Captain John Lovewell of Dunstable determined to stop

this warfare. He made two attempts in the winters of 1723 and 1724 without finding the Indians. Finally in May, 1725, with forty-six experienced scouts, he tramped into the Saco Valley where he met eighty Indians near the lake that now bears his name.

An all-day battle in the woods ended the danger from Abanaki Indians. Captain Lovewell was killed, Paugus was shot, and only twenty Indians survived to admit defeat and retreat to Canada. About half of the scouts lived to return to Dunstable.

The Saco Valley with the broad meadows now in Conway, and the shores of the lakes were uninhabited for the following twenty years. Thus the last of the Abanaki tribes vanished from New Hampshire in 1725.

THE SEAPORT OF PORTSMOUTH

By the turn of the eighteenth century the original fishing village at Strawbery Banke had developed into a busy industrial town and seaport. Its deep and wide harbor rivaled Boston and it was a day's sail nearer to Europe.

The banks of the river and several islands were covered with shipyards which were launching scores of vessels that swelled trading with England and the West Indies and regardless of the Navigation Laws, merchants were buying and selling in the ports of European nations.

Newcastle became a separate town on Great Island in 1693 and Greenland in 1694 yet Portsmouth numbered over two thousand inhabitants. Because the people at Newington objected to walking six miles to church in Portsmouth, a separate parish was established for them. A meetinghouse was erected in 1712 and since the first Sabbath in January 1713, a service of worship has assembled there every Sunday under the same parish society.

Such names as Pickering, Atkinson, Weare, and Vaughn became prominent, but most influential were the Wentworths. In England the family held estates during six previous centuries. William Wentworth, a Puritan closely associated with Oliver Cromwell, arrived in Boston in 1639, removed to Exeter, and was known in Dover as Elder Wentworth.

A descendant, Samuel Wentworth, erected a three-story tavern at the North End in Portsmouth where he was permitted to sell malt liquors. His son John was a shipbuilder who lived in his father's tavern with his wife and sixteen children. His second son John was appointed lieutenant governor of the province of New Hampshire in 1724. His daughter Sarah married a wealthy shipping merchant named Archibald MacPhaedris, a Scotchman, who immediately began to erect for his bride the first residence in New England of Georgian architecture, so named in honor of the king of England.

The walls, eighteen inches thick, were of bricks that he brought from Holland as ballast in his trading ships. The original double gables of this three-story structure were connected later by a flat roof that was surrounded by a balustrade. The owner often climbed his three staircases to stand on this roof while he watched for the return of his ships as they entered the harbor.

Trader MacPhaedris became the owner of a deposit of bog iron in the Lamprey River's bend and the hardware of his home was of bog iron. He offered the iron workers in Scotland twelve acres if they would emigrate to New Hampshire to work his mine.

The walls of the central hall were covered with oil paintings of various designs, of which one was a group of Indians with whom he managed to retain friendly relations in a busy fur trade.

The walls of the rooms and the woodwork were decorated with the latest methods. Hanging there were five portraits by the famous English artist Blackburn. One was a likeness of Sarah Wentworth in a voluminous satin gown and another of their daughter Mary in a blue velvet dress.

Mary married Jonathan Warner, a member of the Governor's Council and a slave owner, as were other of the wealthy families in Portsmouth. Benjamin Franklin was permitted to install a lightning rod upon the southwest corner of the roof of this famous house which remained in the possession of the Warner family until 1931. The Warner House is now open to the public and is well worth a trip to Portsmouth for a visit.

Governor Wentworth's administration was disturbed by a violent earthquake in 1727 that toppled chimneys at the ridgepole although the two-story houses did not fall because of their heavy framework fastened by wooden pins that could shake violently.

Another disaster was an epidemic of "the throat distemper" (probably diphtheria). Youths under twenty were victims. Kingston was widely afflicted with several families losing every child.

Smallpox was also prevalent everywhere. Experience in Portsmouth revealed that persons in excellent health suffered only a milder form of this disease. A small island near the mouth of the Piscataqua River was called Pest Island and still is; it was reserved for so-called "pox parties."

Groups of friends in good health would become exposed to this disease at the island and remain there while enduring a mild case that rendered them immune and did not disfigure the skin as a severe case usually did.

Only by recalling the former conditions do we realize the miracles of medical science of our day.

Governor Benning Wentworth, from a portrait by Blackborn

{3}

A Royal Province

EARLY TOWN GRANTS

A century had passed since Pannaway was settled in 1623 while the population in the four original towns increased by some five thousand inhabitants.

The hunting grounds of the Abanaki Indians, north of Amoskeag Falls and westward into the Connecticut Valley, were a gloomy forest that was claimed by the kings of England and France who fought King George's War and the Seven Years' French and Indian War before these claims were decided in 1763. Nobody actually owned an inch of this territory in New Hampshire and Vermont, that later was known as New Hampshire grants.

A wealthy shipbuilder named John Wentworth was appointed lieutenant governor of New Hampshire in 1724. He sent men to cut a path that would accommodate a two-wheeled ox cart from Kingston, a town that was claimed by New Hampshire and Massachusetts, westward to a new town named Chester.

To obtain a grant for a town a group of men called proprietors formed a corporation in which each paid an equal amount of money for each share of a certain number of acres. This money paid for surveying, roads, bridges, a meetinghouse, and the annual salary for a minister. Since land was the only means for investments, wealthy men bought shares in more than one town, with the intention of selling their acres to pioneer farmers.

Along the banks of the rivers were wide, treeless meadows and the soil beneath the trees of the forest was a deep, fertile leaf mold. Many young men became proprietors while others preferred to select their acres and purchased them from the original proprietor.

There was only one obstacle—the French sent the Iroquois Indians to destroy the English settlers.

Penacook, now Concord, was granted in 1727 although a few men who were there earlier had constructed a log meetinghouse. Parson Walker and several families from Massachusetts began a village but the Iroquois were so menacing that a stockade was built around their homes. The frame of the parson's house still stands on North Main Street in Concord.

On the Sabbath the minister delivered his two long sermons with his loaded gun leaning against the pulpit while the men listened with their loaded guns across their knees.

Records at Concord tell of numerous garrisons where ninety families were assigned shelter in 1746 and a company of militia was maintained for guards, which indicates the constant danger in the Merrimack Valley.

The same conditions existed at Canterbury which was granted in 1727. So-called forts were maintained for refuge. History tells how women returned to cook in their kitchens but were ready to flee at a moment's warning.

After six years Governor Wentworth died and his successor, Jonathan Belcher, granted twenty-one townships, although no inhabitants were ready to occupy them.

The wide, fertile meadows of the Connecticut Valley were eventually claimed by families who took the risk of attacks. Four towns were given numbers from one to four. Block houses were erected to shelter the families when warnings told that Indians were near. In later years these numbers became Chesterfield, Westmoreland, Walpole, and Charlestown.

Across the forest that was once the Sunapee Trail of the Penacook tribe when the hunters gathered, spring and fall, to kill the wild geese on their flights, a line of block houses was built as a barrier against the Indians. Here bands of scouts were maintained to warn the towns of approaching Iroquois.

An abandoned hamlet, known as Danzig, is along this

trail, its cellar holes, pounds, and a few graves telling that families existed there long ago.

Today we may forget that 250 years ago the southern section of the province of New Hampshire was in desperate danger from attacks by the French or by Iroquois Indians. Histories list 190 garrison houses that were maintained by families for safety.

In addition, at least nineteen forts had been erected, some of them protected by cannons that were imported from England. At Star Island, on the Isles of Shoals, a fort was built in 1656, and another at Newcastle at the mouth of the Piscataqua River in 1666. Both forts were armed with cannon. During the French and Indian War in 1745, the fort at Star Island was repaired and mounted with nine four-pounders. Pirates and French privateers menaced these two forts.

The wide, treeless meadows along the banks of the Merrimack and Connecticut rivers were eagerly occupied by brave young families whose safety depended on an accurate aim with a trusty musket.

THE SCOTCH-IRISH

Before the boundary line between New Hampshire and Massachusetts was determined in 1741, both colonies claimed the territory that is now in New Hampshire. In the year 1719 Massachusetts sold twenty square miles, then called Nutfield, to the Reverend James MacGregor, a Scotch-Irish clergyman.

The Scotch-Irish were Presbyterians, a strict sect of the Puritans, who fled from persecution during the reign of James I to Ulster County in northern Ireland.

Because of their religious doctrines and poor economic conditions these Scotch Presbyterians were again fleeing—this time to New England in 1718.

Reverend MacGregor led fifty-six Scotch-Irish families to Nutfield; an intelligent, industrious, and honest group of im-

migrants who soon changed the name Nutfield to Londonderry in memory of their former home in Ireland. Later one
section was called Derry and one Manchester.

Reverend MacGregor purchased much more valuable
property than he comprehended, for here were the fishing
rights to which the Indians had given the name of Amoskeag, meaning salmon, and also shad, alewives, and eels
that came from the sea up the river in the spring.

These immigrants brought two valuable contributions to
New Hampshire. The first was the Irish potato, given this
name because the plant became the staple food of Ireland.
Tradition states that when Sir Walter Raleigh was in Virginia in 1584 he learned about the potato.

Sir Walter carried the plant to England where it was
planted and grew upon its vines small green balls which
had such a disagreeable flavor when cooked and eaten that
the plants were uprooted, thus discovering the real potato
for the British Isles.

The exact spot where the first potatoes were grown in
Derry is disputed, although a large sign that is displayed
upon the Murdock Farm claims this honor.

The second contribution was the small flax wheel. Flax
was grown in New Hampshire but the Scotch-Irish introduced the linen industry when they brought their flax
wheels to Londonderry.

The process of preparing the flax plant for linen thread is
still demonstrated at Old Fort Number Four in Charlestown
on the Muster Days.

The Indians did not molest Londonderry because Reverend MacGregor was a graduate of the same university in
France as was the governor of Quebec and they were close
friends. The Indians were told that the Scotch-Irish were
friends.

Nevertheless, Reverend MacGregor's home was surrounded by a stockade and several garrison houses were erected
in Derry.

Archibald Stark was born in Glasgow, Scotland, in 1689

and became a graduate of Glasgow University before he removed to Ireland and there married Eleanor Nichols. They
sailed to Maine in 1720 with two children who died of smallpox on the voyage. They arrived in Londonderry in 1721.
Their home in Derry burned in 1736 and Archibald purchased 800 acres in what is now Manchester and erected his
small, one-story home above the Amoskeag Falls where he
protected the fishing rights of his townsmen of Londonderry from the fishermen of Massachusetts who came in
large numbers to fish in the spring. There were seven children in the family, and while Archibald and the boys
fished, Eleanor and the girls salted fish by the barrel.

Many more families came to New Hampshire from Ireland to settle towns named Dublin and Peterborough in
memory of former homes.

In 1937 the Amoskeag Industries, Inc., deeded the lot of
sixty-by-ninety feet and the original house to the Molly
Stark Chapter of The Daughters of the American Revolution.

Archibald built his home above the falls and there it
stood until October, 1968, when a much larger, new bridge
was constructed that required the space where the house
had stood since 1736, the oldest house in Manchester.

The State Highway Department removed the house to
2000 Elm Street on a corner lot with many trees behind it
and Ray Brook running along the south border.

Within this ancient house, without the aid of schools,
Archibald Stark educated his sons to read the best books of
English literature of their day. "Live free or die" was an
inheritance from sterling ancestors that John Stark bequeathed to New Hampshire.

A ROYAL PROVINCE

Although fear of raids by Indians was widespread, the
economy of the province was increasing in 1730. The farms
were producing food and clothing. Shipyards were spread-

ing along the banks of the rivers and over the islands in the Piscataqua River. Saw and gristmills and tanneries were busy.

Two-story homes were erected with their long ells connecting to barns and storehouses, surrounded by orchards. Wealthy families employed cooks and housemaids in their kitchens and Negro slaves for butlers and stableboys to care for their riding horses and elaborate coaches.

Public schools were available for all boys and girls and private preparation for those destined for Harvard. Markets flourished. Bridle paths and narrow oxcart roads connected the towns and everyone rode horseback. The Puritan Sabbath was observed in every town meetinghouse.

European clothing was imported for the wealthy classes who enjoyed social life in their homes and at the taverns.

Puritan eyebrows must have been raised when the news was announced that the English Society for the Propagation of the Gospel in Foreign Parts intended to erect an Anglican Chapel in Portsmouth in 1732. Mr. Hope of London had purchased a site on the ridge above Daniel Street with space for a surrounding cemetery as was the custom in England.

Since the Sabbath in 1631 when Parson Moody was banished to the Isles of Shoals because he was "entirely addicted" to the Anglican Church (Episcopal) and had conducted a service using the ritual of the English service, only the Puritan faith had been practiced in New Hampshire.

The building was named Queen's Chapel in honor of Queen Catherine who immediately presented a set of Communion Plate, a robe of heavy purple silk and another the color of gold for the rector, and a Vinegar Bible, as it is known today. (Before the error was detected, forty Bibles were printed with the word vinegar in place of vineyard. Thirty-six copies were burned but four had disappeared, one of these the gift of the queen.)

A special pew for the governor was placed at the right of the chancel, raised two steps above the floor, with a red carpet and a canopy hung with red velvet draperies. The queen added two carved chairs upholstered in red damask.

Immediately many of the distinguished families became communicants at Queen's Chapel where the Reverend Arthur Brown was installed as rector.

About 1740 the old dispute about the boundary line between New Hampshire and Massachusetts was revived. A descendant of John Mason demanded rents. Then taxes were demanded by Massachusetts from farmers who had paid taxes in New Hampshire and believed that they were living there.

A few men paid the double taxes to avoid trouble. When others refused, Massachusetts arrested them and confined them in the jail at Salem. The king then decreed that beginning at three miles north of the mouth of the Merrimack River, the boundary line should run to the Pawtucket Falls, then extend west to the boundary of the province of New York. This placed twenty-one towns in New Hampshire, among them Kingston, Derry, and Salem, and New Hampshire questioned the right of these towns to send their delegates to the assembly (legislature) at Portsmouth.

The colonies became irritated when the king began to increase the duties upon goods that were imported into the colonies. Manufacturing of cloth and metals was forbidden in the colonies; only homespun goods were allowed.

In 1741 the king decided to appoint governors in the colonies and New Hampshire became a royal province. The Wentworth family was influential and a son of the former lieutenant governor was appointed the first royal governor, Benning Wentworth. He was then bankrupt because he had sold a consignment of lumber to Spain which that nation refused to pay for.

Benning Wentworth accepted an impossible position. If he pleased the king, he displeased the colony. He used caution and soon ironed out the problem of representatives to the legislature.

The third war between England and France began in 1744 and drew the colony into increasing trouble with the Iroquois Indians. Trade decreased because of the restrictions of England and money became scarce.

Governor Wentworth was interested in granting new townships and sent surveyors to plan them six miles square. He erected a home at Little Harbor to the south of Portsmouth that contained fifty-two rooms and a stable for thirty horses. At present the house is surrounded by tall lilac shrubs that are reported to be the first planted in New Hampshire.

His home now belongs to the state and is open to the public in the summer months.

GOVERNOR BENNING WENTWORTH

The Hundred Years' War ended in the colonies in 1759 although the Treaty of Paris was not concluded until 1763. The Mother Country achieved her goal of becoming the most powerful nation in the world, yet she acquired, at the same time, a debt of one hundred fifty million pounds.

Now the fertile meadows along the northern rivers were free from danger and many young farmers were eager for land. Governor Benning Wentworth cooperated by sending a surveyor, John McDuffee, to block out townships, six miles square, to be granted to proprietors.

While he was governor, he granted seventy-eight towns, several of them across the Connecticut River in the New Hampshire grants. He made one mistake by retaining, unfortunately, five hundred acres within each town for his "governor's farm." Where three or four towns joined at their boundaries he owned fifteen hundred to two thousand acres in one farm.

John Hazen of Haverhill, New Hampshire, appealed to Governor Wentworth and the Assembly for a road from Coos to the sea to transport the abundant harvests to southern markets. The second province road was immediately authorized, named Coos Road, from Haverhill in a diagonal direction to Durham Falls, a distance of about one hundred miles. The Assembly voted that every landowner was obliged to clear this pathway through his property or forfeit his right.

This road was cleared for wagons in 1768 and by records in State Papers, one hundred twenty-five owners lost their rights. John Sullivan erected storehouses along the bank of the Oyster River in Durham to shelter the products from the north until they could be sent by boats to the markets in Portsmouth, because the roads across the swamps along the shore had not been constructed at that time.

During the following eighty years, until railroads, the Coos Road farm products were transported in wagons drawn by four to eight horses, and the road was slowly traveled by herds of cattle and sheep and flocks of turkeys going to market.

Peace and prosperity would have prevailed if the king and his councilors had not aroused dissension within the thirteen colonies. They claimed that England was obliged to maintain thousands of troops in the colonies to protect them from the French during the Hundred Years' War. Therefore, the colonies should assist in paying the debts.

The colonies replied that this was a contest between England and France in which the colonies should not have been involved, yet they had furnished thousands of troops, scouts, and guards for their own protection and, as a result, were also in debt.

The king refused to listen. The colonies must pay taxes to England. The Navigation Laws that had prevailed since 1660 increased the duties upon both imports and exports to the colonies. Manufacturing in the colonies was forbidden and all goods, whether manufactured in England or not, must be shipped from England in English vessels manned by crews of English sailors. Thus all prices and duties were fixed in England.

The colonies retaliated by ceasing to trade in England. Rich and poor existed with the products of the colonies. This caused such protests from the merchants in England who depended upon the trade from the colonies that the Navigation Laws were repealed.

Then the Stamp Act was enacted which required that all legal papers, newspapers, bills, and some other forms must bear a stamp of varying denominations.

The Portsmouth Gazette had been published the past ten years in Portsmouth. Newspapers were loud in their protests but the stamps were printed in England and deputies were sent to sell them in the colonies.

When the deputy arrived at Portsmouth, he was not permitted to come ashore until he resigned his office. Neither was he allowed to land his stamps. The indignation became so intense that Benjamin Franklin, who was then in London, was invited to speak in the House of Commons. He sadly advised that England would lose the colonies. This caused such consternation that the Stamp Act was repealed before it existed a year.

Suddenly the king discovered in 1766 the acres that Governor Wentworth claimed for himself in New Hampshire. He was immediately removed from his office after serving faithfully over a period of twenty-five years. However, through the influence of his nephew, John Wentworth, who was a favorite of the king, he was permitted to resign.

Governor Wentworth became beloved in New Hampshire. He refused to participate in the controversy with the king but remained neutral in his attitude, which apparently displeased the king.

THE GOVERNOR'S LADY

A portrait of Governor Benning Wentworth by the English artist Blackburn now hangs above the staircase in the Historical Library. His dignified appearance arrayed in the costume of his day may cause one to forget that he was an individual with very human characteristics.

He was one of the older of Lieutenant John Wentworth's sixteen children, born in the three-story mansion that his grandfather erected in the outskirts of Portsmouth. He attended the school of Major Hale to prepare for Harvard, from which he graduated. He became active in the shipping business of the Wentworth family and made three trips to England in the interests of this mercantile trade, voyages that required at least twenty weeks to make the round trip.

He married and had three sons while residing in the old Wentworth mansion. After he became governor, he erected a fifty-two room house at Little Harbor in 1750. The dreaded disease of "throat distemper" did not spare rich or poor and his wife and three sons were claimed in a severe epidemic.

Meanwhile an orphan girl named Martha Hilton was playing around on Court Street one day when a matron chided her for her lively pranks. She replied, "You may scold me now, but some day you will see me riding in my coach." Certainly Martha had her ambitions.

As was the custom, she lived with whatever family would take her in for the little work that she might accomplish. Doubtless she attended public schools as the children of Portsmouth were permitted.

Nothing further is known about Martha until she had developed into an attractive maiden and was employed as a housemaid in the governor's mansion at Little Harbor.

Evidently Governor Wentworth was lonely, for he offered his hand to one of the most attractive young women, Molly Pitman, but Molly preferred a young suitor to becoming the governor's lady.

How Martha attracted the attention of the governor is not known. He became so infatuated that he apparently cared nothing for the opinions of others. He decided to marry his attractive housemaid.

The story about his wedding is authentic history. One day after his councilors and other officials were assembled in his large council chamber, Martha entered the room dressed in a silk gown. The governor took her hand and is said to have commanded the Reverend Arthur Brown to read the marriage ritual. The astonished rector of Queen's Chapel obeyed and soon the housemaid became Lady Benning Wentworth.

When Benning Wentworth became governor of the province, he evidently desired to retire at times to a farm that he acquired on an island in Island Pond, a sheet of water some forty miles southwest of Portsmouth that is bounded by the towns of Hampstead, Salem, and Derry. He surrounded the house with a high stone wall that was fitted with a strong gateway.

The active, young Martha found Birch Farm a lonely summer resort. When an invitation was received from their neighbors to attend an evening gathering, she was delighted. However, the governor immediately declined the invitation and forbade Martha to attend the event.

The dutiful wife accepted his royal decree quietly and probably the governor forgot the affair, for as was his custom, he retired early and was soon asleep. Then Martha slipped out the gate without being observed and attended the party.

As might be expected, the governor missed his companion and awoke to inquire of his servant about her absence. When nobody knew where to find her, the temper of the husband became intensely hot. He gave orders to fasten the gate securely and leave Mistress Martha to herself.

Later in the night several piercing screams were heard. The frightened household ran out to the gate. The governor caught up his robe as he hurried out.

By the dim light of candles the grounds were searched and on the shore of the pond Martha's cloak and dress were found. Realizing that nothing could be learned until morning, full of remorse for his anger, the governor, sad and chilled with cold, returned to his bedchamber.

He found Martha snugly in her bed, apparently asleep. In his joy he forgot to scold, and the tale says that they lived happily ever after.

As the years passed a baby boy was born. After the governor was dismissed, his health failed and Martha was constantly his comfort until his death. She was a dignified Lady Wentworth and people frequently saw her riding in her coach.

The fortune of the governor was large and his relatives

anticipated legacies. Instead, in his will his entire fortune
was bequeathed to Martha and their son. But the money remained in the Wentworth family when an English Michael
Wentworth arrived and later married Martha. He was a
skilled violinist and often accompanied the orchestra at the
cotillions at Stoodley's Tavern.

THE CAPTURE OF LOUISBURG

In the continuing battle between England and the
colonies versus the French and Indians, this time known as
King George's War, the men of Portsmouth played an important part.

On the island of Cape Breton the impregnable French
stronghold of Louisburg was catured in 1745 in the following manner. William Vaughn of Portsmouth proposed
that the colonies attempt it. The troops were mostly from
New England with William Pepperell of Kittery in command.

Sixty ships filled with provisions and twenty-one great
guns sailed in April for the Island of Canso where they
were held for three weeks by ice. On April 30 they boldly
sailed into the harbor at Louisburg. The men immediately
landed and chased one hundred French soldiers into the
woods.

Vaughn sailed up to the harbor and discovered that the
warehouses of the French were outside of the walls of the
fort. These he set on fire and a strong wind blew the smoke
into the fort. This so disturbed the garrison that the commander spiked his guns, barricaded the gates, and took his
100 men over the drawbridge into the walled town.

When he found a small aperture in the wall of the fort,
Vaughn paid an Indian to press through it and open the
gates. When the English were within the fort, a note was
sent to the commander saying that by the "Grace of God
the Fort was taken," and demanded surrender.

Since the supplies were burned and a French frigate bringing more food was surrounded by the English boats, the stronghold of Louisburg was captured without firing a gun.

THE ATTACK ON FORT NUMBER FOUR

Four towns in the Connecticut Valley were numbered one, two, three, and four. The latter is now the town of Charlestown.

The meadows were so fertile that ten families from Massachusetts began to build a village at Number Four in 1735 although they risked attacks by French and Iroquois who were determined to prevent English settlements in the Connecticut Valley. The leader, Captain Phineas Stevens, had been a captive among Iroquois when a lad of seventeen and knew their customs.

The settlers decided that a fort was a necessity and pooled £300 for this purpose. They cut the trees from a wide area above the bank of the river and sawed hundreds of the logs about twelve feet in length to make a stockade. In the center of a clearing a cabin was set at each of the four corners of a rectangle and one at the center of the two long sides. The cabins of Captain Stevens and Dr. Hastings occupied the front or south corners and between them a two-story garrison house was erected with a high watchtower beside the gateway.

The stockade of logs connected the cabins on three sides of the rectangle with its logs spaced so that the muskets could protrude between them. Two wells were dug within the rectangle and one outside the gate. Lean-to roofs at the stockade connected to the roofs of the cabins to provide shelter for the families who still lived outside of the fort when danger was evident—which occurred in the summer season frequently. In the winter the garrison house protected everyone.

This fort was a stronghold during the following forty

years. When no longer needed, it was removed and today its site is covered by the residences of citizens of Charlestown. A replica has been erected north of the village by the Old Fort Number Four Associates.

In the fall of 1746 conditions at the fort became so hazardous that the families with their cattle removed to greater safety further south and the fort was closed for the winter.

In the last week of March, 1747, the governor of Massachusetts authorized Captain Stevens to enlist sufficiently experienced scouts to open the fort. Thirty men of unquestioned courage began to prepare for an anticipated attack.

Early in the morning of April 7 the dogs began to be restless and the guard accompanied them outside the gate. Immediately three Frenchmen opened fire. The guard zigzagged to the gate but was slightly wounded as he entered. Whether the dogs did the same is not on record.

Seven hundred French and Iroquois rained bullets upon the fort incessantly. A cart discovered at the village mill was filled with combustibles and pushed, burning, against the stockade but the guards stationed in the tower proved to be too accurate marksmen to permit this to succeed.

On the second morning under a flag of truce, Frenchmen asked to buy food. Captain Stevens said he was forbidden to sell food. The French were unable to estimate the number within the fort. They had no means of caring for wounded if an assault was risked.

The ice on the river which had been the pathway might break at any moment. On the third morning the commander of the French appeared under a flag of truce to demand surrender. He received a shout of "Never."

The cold, hungry enemy withdrew before night. Captain Stevens sent the message to Boston that the fort was safe. Commander Charles Knowls of troops that the king had sent to Boston sent a sword with a silver hilt to Captain Stevens with a request that the town be named Charlestown in his honor, and troops of English soldiers were assigned to protect the fort during the remainder of King George's War. The families returned to Charlestown to live during the war.

EXPLOITS OF JOHN STARK, SCOUT

Benning Wentworth was a busy governor. Records in the New Hampshire State Papers report that in 1744 he "Impowered four men to mark out a road from Connecticut, due east to Merrimack." This followed the old trail that the Penacook traveled to Lake Sunapee. Over this rough path cannon were dragged to protect Fort Number Four.

A line of block houses was erected along this road and the province paid scouts to continually guard its entire length. In 1748 the governor granted the two towns of Meredith and Holderness, that were north of this line, extensive tracts that are now divided into several towns.

To provide protection from Iroquois, a blockhouse was built in Meredith beside a lake and beneath a large white oak tree, known as the White Oak Blockhouse. Today this name clings to White Oak Lake yet the site of the blockhouse is forgotten.

The first settler in Holderness was a Scot named Samuel Shepard who erected his home not far from Little Squam Lake and a large barn with an original plan for the frame that stands today as firmly as when he raised it about 1751.

Governor Wentworth continued to send scouts to explore northward. In the summer of 1752 two sons of Archibald Stark of Amoskeag Falls, William and John, and Amos Eastman and David Stinson of Dunbarton were scouting and hunting on the Baker River not far distant from the spot where Thomas Baker destroyed the village of the Pemigewasset Indians in 1712.

John, who was born at Derryfield August 28, 1728, was now twenty-four years of age. He had lived at Amoskeag Falls since 1736 where he learned to salmon fish and to work in his father's sawmill, but his real pleasure was hunting.

These four scouts had trapped furs to the value of £550 sterling when they saw tracks of Iroquois. John hurried to gather their traps when the savages attacked. Stinson and

William Stark were in a canoe on the river. Stinson was killed. John struck the Indian's gun aimed at William and motioned him to escape. Meanwhile he endured a beating from the angry Indian.

John and Amos Eastman were taken to the village of St. Francis in Canada as were their valuable furs. There the two prisoners were tested by running the gauntlet.

Amos took a beating from the clubs of the Indians, but John was wiser. He ran swiftly against the first Indian in the line, grabbed his club, and rushed ahead swinging the club right and left. The old Indians were delighted and the sachem adopted John into the tribe.

John kept his eyes and ears open to observe the customs and to learn the language before the captives were rescued. The governor of Massachusetts sent Captain Stevens and Mr. Wheelwright to search for captives with money for ransom. The Iroquois accepted $60 for Amos but refused to sell John until Captain Stevens offered his pony, which proved too tempting to refuse.

Governor Wentworth decided to send explorers up the Connecticut River with scouts from Dunbarton. Knowing that John Stark had traveled there when a captive, he was asked to be a guide. Caleb Page was one of the group and when John met Elizabeth Page, his daughter, he lost his heart immediately.

Within the interim between 1744 and 1756 two events occurred that are worthy of notice.

In Glasgow, Scotland, a teenaged boy who possessed a keen power of observation, sat beside the fireplace waiting for the kettle to boil for tea. He noticed a clicking sound, then saw the lid of the kettle move. The faster the water became steam, the higher the lid was lifting. Here was power. In 1758 James Watts had invented his steam engine.

In 1751 Benjamin Franklin was flying a kite while a thunderstorm was gathering. He noticed that the fibers of the string of the kite were moving. He tapped a steel key that was attached to the string and sparks appeared.

At the Warner House at Portsmouth in 1762, Benjamin

Franklin was installing his lightning rod at one corner of the roof.

The poet Tennyson expressed his philosophy: "Yet I doubt not through the ages one increasing purpose runs,/And the thoughts of men are widen'd with the process of the suns."

THE DURABLE
ELIZABETH PAGE STARK

The famous Molly Stark was born in Haverhill, Massachusetts, on February 16, 1737. She was the fifth child of Caleb and Elizabeth (Merrill) Page.

Haverhill, situated on the bank of the Merrimack River, suffered frequently from attacks by Indians. Probably Elizabeth attended a school and her education included the skill to handle a gun.

Captain Caleb Page removed to Dunbarton in 1752 with his family when Molly was fifteen years of age. The grant belonged to Archibald Stark and was named in honor of Dunbarton Castle in Scotland, his native home. The first famous exploit for Molly was when a bear was known to be near. She went hunting and killed the animal.

In 1752 John Stark was captured by Iroquois Indians and taken to Canada by a route up the Connecticut Valley never traveled by white men. After he was rescued, his reports of this valley became famous, with the result that when Captain Page was authorized to find a guide for an exploring company, John Stark was called to Dunbarton to lead the way for the soldiers.

Molly was a brown-eyed, small girl of seventeen years. John lost his heart immediately and, although usually a silent fellow, he told stories to Molly and Mary Page about his experiences among the Indians.

Molly's eldest brother, Caleb, Jr., became an ensign in Robert Rogers' Rangers and John Stark was appointed second lieutenant. At times the two Rangers came to Dunbarton which permitted John an opportunity to offer his affections to Molly with uncertain favor.

Archibald Stark died soon after and John obtained a leave of absence to return home to settle his father's estate.

When his father's will was probated John rode on horseback to Molly's home and without dismounting said, "If you are ever to become my wife, Molly, you will have to come with me now."

Molly did not hesitate. They were married on August 20, 1758, when John was thirty and Molly twenty-one.

When the war closed, John returned to Dunbarton to the spacious farmhouse where Caleb Page kept his wealth in a half bushel box beneath his bed.

The life was too quiet for restless John. To his satisfaction he was soon ordered to build the Crown Point Road from Charlestown to Fort Fredrick.

During his absence Molly's first child was born on December 3, 1759; she named him Caleb. This baby restored his grandfather's spirits. John and Molly went to live with his widowed mother in the little red house beside the falls in Derryfield but left little Caleb with his grandfather.

John's mother was Scotch-Irish. She preferred porridge made with barley. Molly's was with beans. Mrs. Stark drank buttermilk, Molly used tea. Mrs. Stark died in 1768.

After two children were born, John decided to build a two-story home about a mile from the falls. Only polished wood was used for the walls and two chimneys provided a fireplace in most of the rooms. Here John and Molly and their eight living children enjoyed life as long as they lived.

John bought the rights to the land that his father willed to his family and worked busily in his sawmill until on the morning of April 19, 1775, a messenger brought the news about the battle of Lexington. John, then commander of the patriots in New England, shut his machinery, went home for a change of clothing, and started for Medford, Massachusetts, where the patriots were assembling.

While he was in camp, Molly rode her horse to carry clothes and food frequently. At the time of the Battle of Bunker Hill on June 17, 1775, it is claimed that Molly was behind the rail fence reloading muskets with young Caleb beside her.

Another time when John's men were ill with smallpox, after the family had been inoculated safely, Molly sent for these men and nursed them back to health.

The summons to his army on August 16, 1777, is well known, "Tonight the American flag floats over yonder hill, or Molly Stark sleeps a widow." This was at the Battle of Bennington and Stark won. He continued to serve during the Revolution until the final surrender at Yorktown on October 19, 1781.

Through all of the years of the war, Molly retained the responsibility for the family and the property. Her signature is preserved on family papers. John Stark was, next to George Washington, the wealthiest officer in the American Army.

Their last (eleventh) child, Sophia, was born on June 21, 1782. One baby girl had died in infancy. Molly lived on for thirty-two years to enjoy her spacious home and family. She died in June 1814. General Stark was feeble yet he continued to live until May 8, 1822.

HARD TIMES IN THE COLONIES

To compare our daily life today with existence in 1750 is impossible. To live without money would be exceedingly difficult, yet this was the condition in 1750 in New Hampshire. The colonies were not permitted to coin money. The imports so greatly exceeded the exports that the colonies were always in debt to English merchants so that crowns, shillings, and sixpence were not coming to New Hampshire.

Not only the Scotch-Irish, but also thousands of Englishmen, were migrating to New Hampshire so that the population doubled about 1750. The only surplus was land within the new towns that Governor Benning Wentworth granted.

The forests provided shelter and fuel; the fertile meadows produced food; from the wool and hides of animals and flax clothing was supplied; and natural resources such as salt, fish, and furs increased the income from the farm.

Every person in the family had his work to do. As soon as a child was able to help, he had his task to perform, if only to carry the large chips from the chopping block to the fireplace.

Trade was by barter with every farm producing something for exchange. Corn, hay, wool, and farm products were always in demand. Teen-aged youths earned many dollars with their lines of traps in the winter. The hides of deer and the fur of fox, mink, and otter sold rapidly. Salt and fish from the sea and potash that was distilled from wood ashes for gunpowder were nature's products.

Waste not, want not, was a household maxim. Every drop of tallow was saved for candles, every scrap of fat was used for lye soap. Nut trees were everywhere: chestnuts, butternuts, shag-bark walnuts, smaller, yet as delicious as the English walnut of today, beechnuts, and bushels of acorns (the last two named provided food for swine in time of famine).

Problems for the farmer were unpredictable. Usually a cold, snowy winter left moisture in the fields that produced an abundant harvest while mild winters brought droughts and a sharp drop in the hay crop. There were pests of worms and grasshoppers with no DDT to exterminate them; when crops failed, no parachutes dropped food for the starving. To send abroad for corn and ship it from overseas required several months. Neighborliness was a virtue to practice everywhere.

The forest still covered thousands of square miles and the broad fields of today were not producing crops, yet the population was steadily increasing.

A diary written between 1739 and 1799 is available at the Historical Library in Concord which provides a personal record worthy of study. It tells that a heavy rain for twenty days in 1740 flooded the meadows, washed away bridges, and caused scarcity of food in 1741. Also a severe epidemic of throat distemper took the lives of scores of young folk.

In 1743 army worms spread completely over fields to devour every green leaf, even the foliage of the trees. Scores of farmers lost their entire crops. Grasshoppers also appeared in other sections.

In 1748 snow was twelve feet deep in Hampton and no traveling was possible except upon snowshoes. The following summer produced a plentiful crop of hay and corn.

A dry summer in 1751 produced so little corn that farms from the new townships in the north came to Hampton begging to buy even a quart of corn at any price. The following year a severe frost the last of August prevented the corn from ripening and again people were begging to buy food. Seed was sent from England to plant the next summer.

Plentiful years followed until 1761 when the "most distressing drought" made provisions exceedingly scant. Forest fires raged until rains came the last of August.

During the winter of 1762, the diary states "Many cattle, horses, swine, and an abundance of sheep and lambs died" for want of food. People from the north country towns "came begging for corn almost in a state of starvation."

Those who possessed corn sold it and depended upon buying it when vessels came from England in March. This famine was of two years duration which allowed time to procure corn from England. Corn sold at three pounds and fifteen shillings per bushel and later at six pounds from the vessel.

In the winter of 1763 the crust over the deep snow froze so that "in March people rode and sledded over the fences and anywhere they wanted to go about ten days." The following year brought plenty again, the diary stated. It also said "The Land is in great Commotion by reason of the Stamp Act."

These excerpts from Deacon Lane's diary prove that the hands that cleared those early farms in New Hampshire encountered many hardships that modern science has eliminated.

THE LAST FRENCH AND INDIAN WAR

The final French and Indian War began in 1756. Known in Europe as the Seven Years' War, it ended the contest between England and France. It was a world war with the two nations maintaining armies in Europe, India, and America.

France had a semicircle of forts that extended from the St. Lawrence River to the mouth of the Mississippi River. Both nations sent trained armies to America. France possessed Iroquois Indian and other tribes for allies while England had her thirteen colonies. This was a decision of a century: which nation should control this continent.

After 250 years memories are dim, yet every family of New England stock can recall tales about when Iroquois Indians attacked the homes of their ancestors. Records state that over seven hundred men, women, and children were murdered in New Hampshire between 1730 and 1760.

Fort Number Four was an important stronghold with General Amherst in command of the English soldiers who fought frequent skirmishes with French and Indians around Lake George and Lake Champlain.

There are two books which are must reading: *Northwest Passage* by Kenneth Roberts and *Robert Rogers of the Rangers* by John R. Cuneo. Both authors assign most of the credit for the protection of New England to Robert Rogers and his Rangers throughout this war.

A Scotch-Irish family with their son Robert, a lad about twelve years of age, emigrated to Penacook in 1730. When warned that Iroquois were near, they fled for the night to Walker's garrison. The following morn on their return to their home they saw the ashes of their cabin and their cattle dead on the ground. Young Robert resolved to learn to fight Iroquois.

He studied the customs of these foes. How they lived in the forest and their cruel tortures. Then he compiled a code of twenty rules that he taught to eight bands of twenty Rangers each. Never walk by groups, not even by twos; place one foot ahead of the other in walking; always find the shelter of a tree when attacked; and many more.

Rogers enlisted in the English Army. His Rangers were provincials. Pay from either source was infrequent and because Rogers always distributed what did arrive, he became deeply in debt.

In the beginning the war favored the French. Braddock's defeat in Ohio introduced a young Virginian into fame, George Washington. Ticonderoga was lost in a battle on snowshoes in January of 1757 when Rogers was wounded and John Stark took command. He walked forty miles at night to call relief for the Rangers who fought in this battle. Thus he made a lasting reputation for endurance and bravery.

Then the tide turned, fort after fort fell to the English until Quebec was besieged. The story of how the English found a narrow pathway up the cliff to the Plains of Abraham is well known. Then Montreal surrendered and only the Iroquois were left to be conquered.

This task was assigned to Rogers who led his Rangers through the pathless forest of northern Vermont and discovered the village of St. Francis with its comfortable wigwams and a chapel that contained valuable symbols of the faith of the Jesuit fathers.

Without being detected, Rogers and his men planned a surprise attack in the night. No Indian or wigwam remained and the Rangers fled into the forest before some of the absent Iroquois returned to find their village completely destroyed.

Without food, the Rangers divided into several groups to return to Fort Number Four. Many died of hunger, disease, and exposure. Rogers and his band arrived at Coos meadows expecting to find food there. Rogers floated a raft down the river to the fort, obtained food, poled the raft up the stream and saved his starving Rangers.

The war continued in Europe until the treaty of Paris was signed in 1763. England won the victory but money was scarce everywhere. The colonies had been allowed to issue paper money to pay their soldiers, but it soon became worthless. The king sent a considerable sum to somewhat stabilize the scrip but the financial condition of the colonies was one of the causes of the American Revolution.

THE FORTITUDE
OF ELIZABETH WEBSTER

David Webster was born in Chester on December 12, 1738. He became a Ranger at nineteen, having proved that with his musket he could hit a silver dollar 300 feet away. At the close of the war he returned to Chester and married Elizabeth Clough, his step-sister just turned sixteen.

While he was tramping along the Pemigewasset River, he saw the mile-wide meadows at present-day Plymouth and wished he owned them. When David heard that a group of pioneers in Hollis were asking for a charter for the town of Plymouth, he removed to Hollis and bargained for the meadows.

In 1763 he joined other young men who went to Plymouth to build log cabins, returning to Hollis for the winter. In the following spring David loaded his oxcart with household necessities, declaring that he would drive his oxen up the trail to Plymouth. He told Elizabeth to follow him toward fall when he would have the cabin ready.

Elizabeth obeyed. In late summer with her few-months-old baby David, she started on horseback on the hundred-mile journey, finding settlers' homes for overnight stops until she was above Franklin.

On her final morning, while wading the Smith River, the horse stumbled and baby David dropped into the stream. Rescued by his mother, cold and wet, they reached the shore. With her flint and steel Elizabeth built a fire to dry their clothing before continuing the journey. She feared this delay for she expected to arrive at Plymouth before sundown.

Although she hurried in the late afternoon, she knew that she must find shelter for the night. As she rode along she saw a high cliff and near its top was a cavelike crevice.

Carefully fastening her horse on the grassy bank, with her baby in her arms, the eighteen-year-old girl climbed the hill to the foot of the cliff and by a roundabout scramble from ledge to ledge she found the cave. Looking up the cliff today, one wonders how she managed the dangerous pathway.

She nursed her baby to a sound sleep and she also was soon soundly sleeping. Suddenly she was awakened by the light of fire above the treetops and the howling of Indians above at the top of the cliff.

Trembling with fright lest the baby should cry or the horse begin to plunge about, she listened to the powwow. Finally the feast finished and the Indians went on their way as sleep came again to the worried mother.

In the morning Elizabeth crept to the top of the cliff to be sure that she was alone and safe. All was quiet. She retrieved her horse and after two hours arrived at the cabin and found David. Not knowing when to expect his wife and baby, he had not worried. When Elizabeth told him her story, although he probably was alarmed, he remarked, "You didn't need to be frightened, the Indians around here are friendly."

In the next twelve years a daughter and five sons were born; two of the boys died young. A tavern, two stories in height, was erected beside the main street of the small village. In 1774 Grafton County was established and a courthouse built opposite the tavern. Elizabeth objected to being obliged to see the whipping post and stocks from the front windows so David gave a site on higher ground and moved the small courthouse at his own expense.

In this same building in 1806, Daniel Webster pleaded against capital punishment for a murderer. For this he earned his first fee but lost the case. The courthouse is now the public library in Plymouth and the oldest public building in northern New Hampshire.

In 1764 David bought two Negro slaves, Cisco and Dinah, for servants in the tavern. Tradition tells that Dinah became a famous cook and a kind nursemaid. These faithful servants are buried in the Trinity Cemetery in Holderness at the foot of David's grave.

David was a captain and later a colonel in the New Hampshire enlisted regiments and served in several campaigns until the close of the Revolution. He was appointed sheriff in 1779 and continued until 1809. He died in 1824.

Elizabeth is a perfect example of thousands of mothers in New Hampshire. She gave birth to and nursed eleven children in a period of twenty-two years. She was a housewife, providing meals for her family and the public in the tavern. From the wool of the sheep she carded, spun, wove, and knitted. She trained her sons in the precept "Honesty is the best policy." To her daughter she said "Cleanliness is next to Godliness." She died in 1809.

To these capable, wise although unlettered mothers, the homes of New Hampshire are an honorable memorial.

GOVERNOR JOHN WENTWORTH

John Stewart Wentworth was born at Portsmouth in 1737, a son of Mark Hunking Wentworth and a brother of Benning. He became the wealthiest shipbuilder and merchant in the province.

Young John graduated at Harvard and joined his father's business. In 1764 he was sent to England by his father where he made friends among the high officials, and even became a friend of King George III, who appointed him to continue the Wentworth dynasty not only as royal governor of the province of New Hampshire but also surveyor of the king's woods with a generous salary.

He sailed home by way of South Carolina and made a leisurely trip through the colonies placing the broad arrow upon the trees for the masts for the king's navy. Before leaving England, he shipped several Arabian horses for his stables at his estate of 4,000 acres in Wolfeboro.

At home he erected a large brick home on Pleasant Street, and on November 11, 1768, married his former sweetheart, Frances Deering, then the widow of Theodore Atkinson, Jr. Although there was some disturbance about taxes in Boston, his province was loyal to the king.

Ambition was high to develop his estate on the shore of Smith Pond in Wolfeboro where he was developing a small village that consisted of cottages for servants, stables for his horses, barns for cattle, a sawmill and a gristmill, carpenter's shop, and storehouses. Now he would erect a mansion suitable for the royal governor. He employed Peter Harrison, the most distinguished architect in New England, to plan the interior, while he designed the outside of the building.

From Portsmouth to the ferry at Newington and on to Dover and Rochester, a road was traveled as far as Stephen Wentworth's tavern. On to Middletown and Brookfield, he employed John Drew and Benjamin Hart to supervise a crew of men to complete the highway to his farm at an expense of £2000, known as the Governor's Road, a distance of fifty miles from Portsmouth.

The mansion was two stories in height with a hip roof, of wooden construction, ninety-nine feet in length and thirty-eight feet in breadth. The east end was entirely given to a state council chamber or dining room and a state ballroom above it, both rooms heated by two large fireplaces. A wide hall extended the width of the house with a divided staircase and the remainder of the house contained spacious living rooms with wainscoting thirty-six inches wide of pine from trees that were cut upon his land.

At the west end was a kitchen. Three chimneys contained six fireplaces on the two floors. Between the house and the lake, now named Wentworth, was a garden of shrubbery and flower beds and in the lake were boats of several shapes and sizes.

The governor was planning to develop a farm of many acres, for he was exceedingly interested in the agriculture of his province, and is said to have contributed greatly to its development during the few years that he remained in office.

The founding of a college was his ambition, to be named Dartmouth in honor of the second Earl of Dartmouth who had promised to contribute a large endowment if the institution should bear his name.

On August 11, 1769, Governor Wentworth granted a charter for Dartmouth College with Reverend Eleazar Wheelock its president. The location was at Hanover and this required a road across the colony between Wolfeboro and Hanover.

Samuel Shepard, first settler of Holderness, was appointed to lay out the Dartmouth College Road between Wolfeboro and Plymouth. The route passed along the Miles Road through the grants of Peter Livius, a member of the Provincial Council, and that of Jonathan Moulton, the nabob of Hampton. The road was "enfenced" because both men cherished a grudge against the governor. Nevertheless, it continued to encircle Squam Lake to the home of Samuel Shepard where the house and a remarkable barn are standing today, and on to Plymouth.

To attend the first commencement at Dartmouth College in 1771, Governor Wentworth and his officials with their servants rode their horses over the Dartmouth College Road from Wolfeboro to Plymouth. They were entertained the first night by Samuel Livermore at Holderness and Parson Ward at Plymouth. Probably David Webster looked after the servants at his tavern in Plymouth. Because the road was not completed to Hanover, they rode over the new Coos Road to Haverhill and down the trail along the Connecticut River to Hanover.

There they saw four men graduate from Dartmouth College. In 1772 and 1773 eight more men graduated with Governor Wentworth in attendance and he traveled over the entire College Road. The last year he was said to have entered Hanover in his coach, a doubtful statement because this pathway was only a bridle path. Mrs. Wheelock may have loaned her coach that she rode into Hanover from Lebanon, Connecticut.

Thus within seven years after he became governor, John Wentworth realized his ambitions to build his estate in Wolfeboro and establish a college in New Hampshire.

In 1774 John Wentworth was torn between two loyalties: his office as royal governor to which the king had appointed him and his native province of New Hampshire.

EXTRAORDINARY.
New Hampfhire Gazette,
OR,
EXETER Morning Chronicle.

[Vol. I.]   TUESDAY, JULY 16, 1776.   [No. 9.]

IN CONGRESS, JULY 4, 1776.

Declaration.

By the REPRESENTATIVES of the UNITED STATES OF AMERICA, In GENERAL CONGRESS Affembled.

WHEN in the Courfe of Human Events, it becomes neceffary for one People to diffolve the Political Bands which have connected them with another, and to affume among the Powers of the Earth, the feperate and equal Station to which the Laws of Nature and of Nature's God entitle them, a decent Refpect to the Opinions of Mankind require that they fhould declare the Caufes which impel them to the Seperation.

We hold thefe Truths to be felf-evident, that all Men are created equal, that they are endowed by their Creator with certain unalienable Rights, that among thefe are Life, Liberty, and the Purfuit of Happinefs. That to fecure thefe Rights, Governments are inftituted among Men, deriving their juft Powers from the confent of the governed, that whenever any Form of Government becomes deftructive of thefe Ends, it is the Right of the People to alter or to abolifh it, & to inftitute new Government, laying its foundation on fuch Principles, and organizing its Powers in fuch Form, as to them fhall feem moft likely to effect their Safety and Happinefs. Prudence, indeed, will dictate that Governments long eftablifhed fhould not be changed for light and tranfient Caufes, and accordingly all Experience hath fhewn, that Mankind are more difpofed to fuffer, while Evils are fufferable, than to right themfelves by abolifhing the Forms to which they are accuftomed —— But when a long Train of Abufes and Ufurpations, purfuing invariably the fame Object, evinces a defign to reduce them under abfolute Defpotifm, it is their Right, it is their Duty, to throw off fuch Government, and to provide new Guards for their future Security. Such has been the patient Sufferance of thefe Colonies ; and fuch is now the Neceffity which conftrains them to alter their former Syftems of Government. The Hiftory of the prefent King of Great-Britain is a Hiftory of repeated Injuries and Ufurpations, all having in direct object the Eftablifhment of an abfolute Tyranny over thefe States. To prove this, let Facts be fubmitted to a candid World.

He has refufed his affent to Laws, the moft wholefome & neceffary for the public Good.

He has forbidden his Governors to pafs Laws of immediate and preffing Importance, unlefs fufpended in their Operation till his Affent fhould be obtained ; and when fo fufpended, he has utterly neglected to attend to them.

He has refufed to pafs other Laws for the Accommodation of large Diftricts of People, unlefs thofe People would relinquifh the Right of Reprefentation in the Legiflature, a right ineftimable to them, and formidable to Tyrants only.

He has called together Legiflative Bodies at Places unufual, uncomfortable, and diftant from the Depofitory of their public Records, for the fole purpofe of fatiguing them into compliance with his Meafures.

He has diffolved Reprefentative Houfes repeatedly, for oppofing with manly firmnefs his Invafions on the Rights of the People.

He has refufed for a long Time, after fuch

Diffolutions, to caufe others to be elected ; whereby the Legiflative Powers, incapable of Annihilation, have returned to the People at large for their exercife ; the State remaining in the mean Time expofed to all the Dangers of Invafion from without, and Convulfions within.

He has endeavoured to prevent the Population of thefe States ; for that purpofe obftructing the Laws for Naturalization of Foreigners ; refufing to pafs others to encourage their Migrations hither, and raifing the Conditions of new appropriations of Lands.

He has obftructed the Adminiftration of Juftice, by refufing his Affent to Laws for eftablifhing judiciary Powers.

He has made Judges dependent on his will alone, for the tenure of their Offices, and the amount and payment of their Salaries.

He has erected a Multitude of new Offices, and fent hither fwarms of Officers to harrafs our People, and eat out their Subftance.

He has kept among us, in Times of Peace, ftanding Armies, without the confent of our Legiflatures.

He has affected to render the Military independent of and fuperior to the Civil Power.

He has combined with others to fubject us to a Jurifdiction foreign to our Conftitution, unacknowledged by our Laws ; given his affent to their Acts of pretended Legiflation.

For quartering large Bodies of armed Troops among us,

For protecting them by a mock Trial, from Punifhment for any Murders which they fhould commit on the Inhabitants of thefe States :

For cutting off our Trade with all Parts of the World :

For impofing Taxes on us without our Confent :

For depriving us, in many Cafes of the Benefits of Trial by Jury :

For tranfporting us beyond Seas to be tried for pretended Offences :

For abolifhing the free Syftem of Englifh Laws, in a neighbouring Province, eftablifhing therein an arbitrary Government, and enlarging its Boundaries, fo as to render it at once an Example and fit Inftrument for introducing the fame abfolute Rule into thefe Colonies :

For taking away our Charters, abolifhing our moft valuable Laws, and altering fundamentally the Forms of our Governments :

For fufpending our own Legiflatures, and declaring themfelves invefted with Power to legiflate for us in all Cafes whatfoever.

He has abdicated Government here, by declaring us out of his Protection, and waging War againft us.

He has plundered our Seas, ravaged our Coafts, burnt our Towns, and deftroyed the Lives of our People.

He is at this Time, tranfporting large Armies of foreign Mercenaries to compleat the Works of Death, Defolation and Tyranny, already begun with Circumftances of Cruelty and Perfidy, fcarcely parallelled in the moft barbarous Ages, and totally unworthy the Head of a civilized Nation.

He has conftrained our fellow Citizens taken Captive on the high Seas to bear Arms againft their Country, to become the Executioners of their Friends and Brethren, or to fall themfelves by their Hands.

He has excited Domeftic Infurrections amongft us, and has endeavoured to bring on the Inhabitants of our Frontiers, the mercilefs Indian Savages, whofe known Rule of Warfare, is an undiftinguifhed Deftruction, of all Ages, Sexes and Conditions.

In every Stage of thefe Oppreffions we have petitioned for Redrefs, in the moft humble Terms : Our repeated Petitions have been anfwered only by repeated Injury. A Prince whofe Character is thus marked by every Act which may define a Tyrant, is unfit to be the Ruler of free People.

Nor have we been wanting in Attention to our Britifh Brethren. We have warned them from Time to Time of Attempts by their Legiflature to extend an unwarrantable Jurifdiction over us. We have reminded them of the Circumftances of our Emigration and Settlement here. We have appealed to their native Juftice and Magnanimity, and we have conjured them by the Ties of common Kindred to difavow thefe Ufurpations, which inevitably interrupt our Connections and Correfpondence. They too have been deaf to the Voice of Juftice and of Confanguinity. We muft therefore acquiefce in the Neceffity which denounces our Separation, and hold them, as we hold the reft of Mankind, Enemies in War ; —— in Peace, Friends.

We, therefore, the Reprefentatives of the UNITED STATES OF AMERICA, in GENERAL CONGRESS affembled, appealing to the Supreme Judge of the World for the Rectitude of our Intentions, do in the Name, and by the Authority of the good People of thefe COLONIES, folemnly Publifh and Declare, that thefe UNITED Colonies are, and of Right ought to be, FREE and INDEPENDENT STATES, that they are abfolved from all Allegiance to the Britifh Crown, and that all political Connection between them and the State of Britain, is and ought to be totally diffolved ;——and that as FREE and INDEPENDENT STATES, they have full Power to levy WAR, conclude PEACE, contract Alliances, eftablifh COMMERCE, and to do all other Acts and THINGS which INDEPENDENT STATES may of Right do. And for the Support of this Declaration, with a firm Reliance on the Protection of Divine Providence, we mutually pledge to each other our Lives, our Fortunes, and our facred Honor.

Signed by Order and in Behalf of the Congrefs,

JOHN HANCOCK, Prefident.

Atteft,

CHARLES THOMPSON, Secretary.

TO BE SOLD

At the Printing-Office on the Grand Country Road, near the State-Houfe in EXETER, THE Manual or 64th EXERCISE, with and without the Cuts —— Pickering's Exercife, with Cuts —— Price's Obfervations on the Nature of Civil Liberty, the Principles of Government, and the Juftice and Policy of the WAR with America ; London printed ; Bofton, Re-printed ; is much admir'd and read. —— COMMON SENSE with large Additions, together with a variety of other fmall Books —— Father Ab-y's Will, and fundry other little Things of the kind. Alfo, Blanks of moft forts, ufed in this Colony—Writing Paper, by the Quire—beft of Dutch Quills—Sealing Wax, &c. &c.

Sold at the Printing-Office in Exeter.

Declaration of independance

First publication in New Hampshire of the Declaration of Independence

{4}

Rebellion
and
Independence

THE PINE TREE RIOT

England was an island kingdom and obliged to maintain a strong navy. Early in the history of the colonies the king appointed a surveyor of the king's woods who marked the white pines that were suitable for masts with the broad arrow which reserved them for the navy.

When the quarrel between France and England began in 1690 King William and Queen Mary enacted a law that all pine trees suitable for masts were reserved for their navy.

In 1722 the legislature of New Hampshire consented to a law that any owner of land must pay a generous license before he cut a pine tree that was twelve inches in diameter at three feet above the ground.

When Governor Benning Wentworth began to grant town charters he reserved all white pines that were suitable for masts for the navy.

Only over a straight, level Mast Road was it possible for forty yoke of oxen to transport one of these pine trees to a shipyard; hence "Mast Road" passing down Route 114 through Weare and Goffstown.

As time passed, the pine tree regulations were not enforced within the inland towns, among them Weare, which Governor Wentworth regranted in 1764 with the name of Weare, in honor of Meshech Weare, popular member of the General Court.

In 1766 King George I appointed John Wentworth to be governor of New Hampshire and also "surveyor of the king's woods" with a generous salary. The new governor, loyal to King George, discovered the old pine tree law of 1722 which would add many pounds to the king's treasury with its license (taxes).

Many deputy pine tree surveyors were appointed who were supposed to visit the forests of each settler and mark the pines that were twelve inches in diameter at three feet above the ground—a rule which the settlers ignored. Deputies waited until the pine trees were cut and in the mill yards where they were easily seen and marked.

Such was the situation in 1772. The governor and his laws had become exceedingly unpopular. A deputy surveyor appeared in the mill yards in Weare and surrounding towns where he discovered hundreds of pine logs of king size. These he marked with the broad arrow. On February 7, 1772, the names of the owners of these logs were published in the *Portsmouth Gazette* with a summons to come to the Admiralty Court and show why their logs should not be forfeited.

The owner of the mill yards sent Samuel Blodgett, a very well known citizen of Goffstown, to settle the business. Governor Wentworth immediately recognized the ability of Mr. Blodgett and persuaded him to accept an appointment as a deputy surveyor.

To the surprise of the owners of the logs, on February 24 they received a letter from Mr. Blodgett saying that he regretted that he must oblige them to come to him and pay for cutting the king's pines, but he would make it easy for them.

The owners of the logs from Goffstown and Bedford immediately settled and kept their logs. The men at Weare knew that they had observed the regulations of their charter and they refused to obey the demands of the Tory Governor Wentworth. They did not meet with Mr. Blodgett. Warrants were given for their arrests to Benjamin Whitting, sheriff of Hillsborough County. On April 23, 1772, with his deputy John Quigilly, the sheriff arrived at Weare late in the afternoon where they engaged rooms for the night at Henry Quimby's tavern. They planned to arrest Ebenezer Mudgett, the biggest offender.

The news spread rapidly. Many citizens went to Mr. Mudgett's home with offers to pay for his bail. However, other plans were made.

Early the following morning Mr. Mudgett arrived at the tavern and rushed into the sheriff's bedroom—saying that he had come to pay his fine.

The sheriff began to dress although expressing objections to the early arrival. Suddenly twenty or more men crowded into the room carrying switches.

The sheriff grabbed his pistol but was disarmed. Two men grasped his arms and two more his legs. Holding him face down above the floor, the other men administered a switching upon his bare back. He said that they nearly killed him.

Naturally the sheriff was angry and demanded action. He sent a number of soldiers to arrest the offenders, but they had fled to the woods.

Finally at the September term of the court eight men were accused by the sheriff. The officers of the court were Theodore Atkinson, Meshech Weare, Leverett Hibbard, and William Parker, all patriots who were in sympathy with the offenders.

All of the eight pleaded guilty and were fined twenty shillings each and the costs of the court, which was the least that the law demanded. The case was dismissed and nothing was done about the logs.

Historians have claimed that had this earlier event been publicized in the *Portsmouth Gazette* as was the Boston Tea Party in the *Boston Newsletter,* this tale of revolt in New Hampshire would be equally famous today.

The plaque marking the site of the "Pine Tree Riot" can be seen in Weare beside Highway 114.

WAR CLOUDS GATHER

Under the influence of Governor John Wentworth the province of New Hampshire remained loyal to the king, although unrest was increasing. The English statesman William Pitt, declared that "Taxation without representation was tyranny." The colonies demanded a voice about taxes.

One of the causes of trouble was a tax of a shilling a gallon upon molasses from the islands in the West Indies that were claimed by the French. This made the price too high for the distilleries in the colonies. Because the British Islands could not produce sufficient sugar and molasses, smuggling was practiced. To prevent smuggling the king issued Writs of Assistance to his deputies which permitted them to search wherever they suspected to find smugglers.

In Boston the deputies were given a coat of tar and feathers by the Sons of Liberty, an organization of patriots who possessed secret passwords and signs. A deputy in New Hampshire became so unpopular that he resigned his office. Smuggling continued.

The usual beverage was made with New England rum and was called "toddy." When the distilleries did not produce rum, trouble arose. Finally all of the duties were repealed except for the ones on tea, glass, and a few other articles.

Fearing that trouble was imminent, the Assembly appointed a Committee of Safety with Meshech Weare the chairman, an experienced and honored citizen and patriot, as they were called to distinguished them from the loyalists who were named Tories. Prominent patriots were John Langdon of Portsmouth, John Sullivan of Durham, Dr. Josiah Bartlett of Kingston, and Nicholas Gilman of Exeter.

The king's attorney was Samuel Livermore. He was born in Waltham, Massachusetts, was a graduate of Princeton (then called Nassau Hall), studied law, and was admitted to the Superior Court of Massachusetts in 1756. He became a citizen at Portsmouth and married the daughter of the Reverend Arthur Brown.

Samuel Livermore was appointed judge advocate of the Admiralty Court with the highest salary in the province which he wisely invested in land. He became the owner of hundreds of acres in Holderness, Campton, Ashland, and Bridgewater.

Because he believed in the patriot's rights, Judge Livermore removed to Derry and later to Holderness where he had sent workmen to construct several houses and a saw and a gristmill.

When Governor John Wentworth wished to consult his attorney general he would ride from Wolfeboro to Holderness where they were accustomed to sit upon the stone wall of a spring while they secretly conferred near the gristmill. Tradition tells that Attorney Livermore would borrow his miller's dusty suit and seem to be too busy to leave his mill.

The governor was a patriot yet he remained loyal to his king. The story is told in Wolfeboro that one day he watched the soldiers of the patriot army ride away with his beloved horses which they had confiscated for the officers to ride. He lost hope for his ambitions for the province of New Hampshire.

The first hostility of the mob at Portsmouth was an attack upon an unpopular Tory named John Fenton. Formerly he had received a grant of hundreds of acres of land in Plymouth that was later divided into farms; one of them is known as the "Tory Farm" today. He owned a farm at the foot of Breed's Hill in Medford, Massachusetts.

When the mob pursued him in Portsmouth, he took refuge in the governor's house on Pleasant Street. A cannon was drawn before the front door and a threat was made to fire it unless the Tory surrendered. When he obeyed, he was jailed. Later he was allowed to sail to Ireland with his wife and three children.

The cannon was not loaded but it served its purpose. A letter written to a friend by Lady Wentworth, now among the State Papers, describes her fears for the safety of her family although the Committee of Safety guarded the home.

At Boston conditions became so hostile in 1768 that the king sent 3,000 troops under command of General Gage to subdue "those rebels" and demanded that the town support this force of men. Many of the inhabitants fled to outer towns.

On March 5, 1770, the Boston Massacre occurred when a

street quarrel caused the king's soldiers to fire into a stone-throwing mob and four men were killed.

The Assembly continued to meet in Portsmouth with thirty-two representatives from the towns. Governor Wentworth was an able official. He was a military man and fifteen regiments with officers were organized within the province. Five counties were established in 1769. In 1773 the population of the towns was reported to the Assembly and the evaluation of the estates. An estimate for the state taxes was begun but the Revolution interrupted the plans of Governor John Wentworth.

THE REVOLUTION—FIRST ACTION

In the middle of December, 1773, a ship sailed into Boston Harbor bringing 342 cases of tea from the East India Company to be sold and taxed at the advice of King George III.

During the evening of December 16, 1773, a group of the Sons of Liberty, disguised as Indians, took possession of the ship, opened the chests of tea, and dumped their contents into Boston Harbor.

The following morning the shore of Dorchester Bay was covered with tea leaves. This treasonable action has become known as The Boston Tea Party.

When another ship was about to enter the harbor at Portsmouth with its cargo of tea, the captain was advised to sail on to Halifax, which he did. In other colonies this same advice was followed.

A barrier was guarded by British soldiers across the narrow strip of land known as The Neck which prevented Boston from becoming an island, and no person was permitted to leave the town. However, one young Son of Liberty knew a secret path across The Neck to a stable where he kept his bay horse. His name was Revere.

Paul Revere was the son of a skilled Huguenot goldsmith and an expert with copper and silver. By his spy system he discovered that General Gage was sending a ship to Fort William and Mary in Portsmouth to bring the store of British gunpowder to Boston.

On the evening of December 13, 1774, Paul Revere stole to his stable, mounted his swift horse, and galloped the forty or more miles over the unknown, rough road to Portsmouth. His horse proved sure-footed through the darkness and about dawn, Paul Revere knocked at the door of John Langdon.

He delivered his news that the British ship was on the way to Portsmouth, then groomed his tired horse and found a bed where he was soon asleep. John Langdon was immediately on the road to Durham to consult with John Sullivan, the young Irish lawyer, who advised action. They hastened to Portsmouth and soon the drum was beating to summon the patriots together.

By sunset John Pickering had a fleet of boats ready to carry four hundred men down the river in the darkness to Fort William and Mary. If one accepts the statement of historians that here was the first action of the American Revolution, then John Pickering has the distinction of becoming the first soldier, when he leaped over the side of his boat, waded ashore, scaled the wall of the fort, and grasped the gun of the surprised guard saying, "You are my prisoner."

The five men at the fort were soon under guard, and ninety-eight barrels of English gunpowder were carried to the boats and floated up the river. When the British boat arrived the following morning, the powder was gone from the fort.

Seventy-two barrels were taken to Exeter and placed in the custody of Nicholas Gilman and several other patriots. The other twenty-six barrels went to Durham where tradition says that John Sullivan concealed a part of them within the closet beneath the pulpit of the meetinghouse.

Legend tells that John Demerrit transported some of this powder in his oxcart to Medford and this was used at Bunker Hill. General "Joe" Cilley of Nottingham received eight barrels. Twelve barrels went to Kingston and six of them went to the army after the Battle of Bunker Hill. General Washington asked for powder and twelve barrels were sent to him at Cambridge.

Records show that one half of this powder was still in New Hampshire after the Battle of Bunker Hill and the remaining supply was sent to Cambridge for Washington's army. English powder contained a greater explosive force than the potash powder and the two were mixed for the army.

In Portsmouth, then a town of over 3,000 inhabitants, hostility toward Tories increased with such rapidity that the Committee of Safety found it difficult to protect the home of Governor Wentworth.

With his wife and son he fled for safety to Fort William and Mary. Later they sailed in a British ship to England and the governor, loyal to his king, never returned to his beloved native New Hampshire.

Years later John Wentworth was appointed governor of Nova Scotia where he served over a period of many years. He died there in 1820. Lady Wentworth and her son made several visits to Portsmouth in the passing years.

The mansion at Wolfeboro burned in 1820. The roof was reshingled and one cold, windy morning a woman filled the large fireplace with the old, dry shingles and set them burning. The strong wind drew burning embers to the roof which caught fire. The beautiful mansion was soon a heap of ashes in the cellar.

The estate, much reduced in area, was deeded to the state of New Hampshire by its last owner, Professor Lawrence Mayo, the author of the excellent biography of John Wentworth.

LEXINGTON, CONCORD,
AND BUNKER HILL

Four months after the powder was taken from Fort William and Mary, General Gage learned that the patriots were storing powder at Concord, Massachusetts. He decided that he would secretly seize that powder.

Accordingly he detailed 800 redcoats to march to Concord on April 18, 1775. But the Sons of Liberty knew of his plans immediately and Paul Revere again rode his bay horse to "spread the alarm" as the Poet Longfellow wrote, "through every Middlesex village and farm."

General Gage knew that Samuel Adams and John Hancock were staying at Lexington and he hoped to capture them on his march. Paul Revere was ahead of his troops and the two leaders of the Sons of Liberty were not staying in Lexington that morning.

When the British troops arrived in Lexington at dawn, fifty patriots were standing on the green. The British officer ordered them to disperse. When they did not obey, somebody fired a gun and more guns fired and eight patriots lay dead on the green while the other forty-two fled. Such was the Battle of Lexington.

The British troops marched on to Concord where more shots were exchanged at the bridge but no powder was discovered for it had been moved elsewhere. Then the British marched back the twenty miles to Boston.

Now, from behind stone walls, trees, and buildings, shots were fired until the lines broke and the soldiers ran in the sun, thirsty and tired. General Gage sent fresh troops to the rescue or all of his men would have been killed. As it was, 293 were shot, while the British managed to kill 93 patriots.

A messenger brought the news of the battle to John Stark in New Hampshire. He went to his home for fresh clothing and food, and rode to Medford, for he had been appointed commander of the volunteers of New Hampshire who were assembling in Medford by hundreds.

All remained quiet, however. Volunteers went home to plant their corn; even Stark returned to represent Derryfield at the session of the legislature in Portsmouth. Men volunteered for short periods at that time.

In June, 1775, the patriots in Boston decided to attempt to drive the British out of Boston. They began to pile earthworks along the top of Bunker Hill and a lower Breeds Hill across the Charles River from Culps Hill in Boston where General Gage had erected his barracks.

Meanwhile reinforcements had arrived from England under command of Lord Howe and Generals Clinton and Burgoyne. Lord Howe took command and ordered that the hills must be taken before the patriots fired cannon into Boston, although he must have known that the patriots did not possess cannon.

On a hot June 17, 1775, 3,000 British troops were equipped with supplies for three days and in their red coats and white trousers and black boots the prize regiment of Welsh Fusileers made an impressive appearance. They marched to Breeds Hill, took off their coats, and ate their lunch as they sat upon the grass. About three o'clock a line was formed that marched up the hill at command of Lord Howe.

The patriots held their fire until the British were within fifty yards, then sent a volley that mowed down the advanced men and the others fled down the hill. A second line advanced and again the line was killed while the rear fled, but when a third line advanced, the patriots had used all of their powder and bullets. The hill was taken while the patriots fled down the hill.

At the foot of the hill, John Stark had realized that this situation would develop. He had taken a rail fence for a barricade, then erected a parallel rail fence several feet away and filled the intervening space with newly cut hay from Tory John Fenton's field which would stop bullets while his men crouched behind the fence.

As the patriots fled down the hill, John Stark's New Hampshire troops covered their retreat and saved the day from a complete disaster. The British lost 1,054 soldiers and the patriots lost 441 and the only result seemed to be to prove that patriots could face trained British soldiers.

Before the battle, teenaged Caleb Stark appeared to his father ready to fight. He sent him to the rear where he is said to have reloaded muskets which required several minutes to accomplish. There is a tradition that his wife Molly was there also loading muskets. She often visited the camp in Medford to bring clothing and food.

Three days before the Battle of Bunker Hill, the Continental Congress in Philadelphia appointed George Washington to be the commander of the American Army for the Revolution. He soon arrived in Cambridge, Massachusetts, and began to "whip the troops into a trained army" which is said to have been an actual fact since whips were used to compel men to obey orders, immediately.

The frustrated General Gage ordered his troops to sail for Halifax and Lord Howe moved to New York in March, 1776.

INDEPENDENCE
AND THE BEGINNING OF WAR

When unrest increased among the colonies, a Committee of Correspondence was organized with John Sullivan and Nathaniel Folsom representing New Hampshire. This committee organized a Continental Congress composed of representatives from all of the colonies chosen in proportion to their population.

New Hampshire appointed three men. Dr. Josiah Bartlett of Kingston was a skilled physician who had discovered a remedy that saved many lives from the dreaded throat distemper; a man of unusual wisdom. William Whipple was a prosperous merchant of Portsmouth who was in later years appointed a judge of the state courts. He understood the problems of the province. Dr. Mathew Thornton was a Scotch-Irishman who arrived in Derry in 1740. He soon became a well-respected citizen and was elected to the Provincial Congress. The three men were loyal patriots.

The first Continental Congress assembled in Philadelphia, Pennsylvania, on September 5, 1774, and remained in session for thirty-two days. This congress discussed the difficulties with the Mother Country, passed resolutions, and adjourned to the following May, 1775.

The second Congress met on May 10, 1775; war was really declared when George Washington was appointed commander of the Continental Army.

Meanwhile a Provincial Congress was elected in New Hampshire, composed of representatives from every town in proportion to every one hundred of the population. This congress met at Exeter in July, 1774 with Meshech Weare as president. A census of the province was authorized that showed the population numbered 82,200 inhabitants. Printing of paper money was voted; the number on the Committee of Safety was increased; twelve members for a Senate were chosen, and six other members appointed for a Council.

The fifth session of this congress declared that New Hampshire was separated from the English government and with the advice of the Continental Congress took the name of The State of New Hampshire. Thus New Hampshire became a state six months before the colonies declared independence. The date should be remembered: December 22, 1775.

Then the naval frigate *Raleigh* was built at Portsmouth, its keel was laid in two months and it mounted thirty-two guns. This is the ship that is displayed upon the state flag and the state seal.

In Philadelphia the Continental Congress debated independence until the thirteen colonies agreed, and on July 4, 1776, the Declaration of Independence was declared. The liberty bell was rung so long and loud that the vibrations cracked the bell metal from the rim to the shoulder.

Thomas Jefferson of Virginia wrote the document probably with the advice of Thomas Paine, a famous author of that day. It would be advisable to reread the text which consists of a preamble, then a statement of twenty-one reasons for separation, and a final reliance upon Divine Providence by which the fifty-six signers mutually pledged to each other their lives, their fortunes, and their sacred honor.

The document was not signed until August 2, 1776. There was no necessity for haste, the news could not arrive in England until a sailing ship could make the voyage of about three months.

The troops in the regiments of New Hampshire joined the army under Washington. Among the famous names to remember are Enoch Poor of Exeter, Joseph Cilley of Nottingham, George Reed of Londonderry, Henry Dearborn of Hampton, and John Sullivan of Durham—all were in the early battles in 1776.

In March, knowing that the men in New Hampshire would follow John Stark, George Washington sent him to the state to enlist more troops.

Stark was at home a few days when he received word that General Enoch Poor had been made a brigadier general. This was intended as an insult to Stark by military men who disliked him because of his positive way of expressing his opinions although he was always in the right.

General Stark should have been given this honor. He was older than General Poor, far more experienced, and he was deeply hurt. On March 22 he appeared at the Provincial Congress in Exeter where he resigned his military position in the army and returned to his home a private citizen. Every effort was made to persuade him to reconsider, by Enoch Poor and many other men, but Stark was adamant.

No man had served more loyally in the French and Indian War as a Ranger, at Bunker Hill, and at Trenton on Christmas night in 1776. His action was justified. He returned to his home and his lumber business which was sadly neglected.

During the winter of 1777 while the American army was cold and hungry at Valley Forge and General Howe and his English Army were warm in New York, King George III was planning to defeat the colonies. He hired thousands of Hessian troops and enlisted more English soldiers to send to Canada in the spring. He intended to separate New England from New York with these troops while General Howe invaded the middle colonies.

THE BATTLE OF BENNINGTON

Early in August, 1777, General Stark at Fort Number Four received a message that General Burgoyne had sent 1,500 troops in command of General Baum, many of them hired Hessians, to pillage New England with orders to find 3,900 horses for the officers to ride and to draw the cannon and supply wagons.

Within three days Stark had equipped his 250 men with food and ammunition and they were on the march toward Bennington, Vermont, where the Green Mountain Boys were storing their supplies.

On the third day, Stark rode into Manchester, Vermont. There he received orders to move his troops across the Hudson River to resist Burgoyne's advance southward toward Saratoga, New York.

Stark refused this order, saying that his men were provincial troops who were paid by New Hampshire and Massachusetts to protect New England and that he would proceed toward the immediate enemy, Baum. When George Washington learned of this disobedience, he reported Stark to the Continental Congress in Philadelphia.

The congress removed Stark's name from the Continental war rolls together with his military titles. Stark continued toward Bennington where he discovered Baum and his troops encamped about eight miles from the town upon a plateau that was surrounded by woods.

Baum had demolished a group of log cabins except one that he left for his headquarters. With the logs, a rampart had been constructed along the slope of the plateau and cannons had been placed upon it.

Stark's army had now increased to 1,600 men from the towns of New Hampshire and Massachusetts. Many companies had officers who had experience in Robert Rogers' Rangers. They camped about a mile below the plateau within the woods.

Stark made his plans to surround Baum's army. Baum was building walls of earth along the two sides of his camp and the forest was at his rear. Stark divided his troops into four sections. He sent 400 men on the right side and 400 others on the left side to go through the woods to surround the plateau. He continuously marched his experienced troops below and in sight of Baum's army, to draw their attention.

About three o'clock on the afternoon of August 16 Baum opened fire. His cannon and musket balls shot limbs off the trees but did no harm to Stark's troops. Before Baum's troops had time to reload, Stark gave his order to "charge."

Rushing up the bank, they leaped the barricade. Tradition tells that Ezekiel Webster, father of Daniel, was the first over the wall, shouting, "Come on, boys. Got to get going!" Baum's troops were surprised. Then followed a hand-to-hand battle with bayonets and muskets during the next hour and a half.

Stark had made his famous challenge before this fight, "Now, my men, yonder are the Hessians, they were bought for seventeen pounds, ten pence a man. Are you worth more? Prove it. Tonight the American flag floats over yonder hill, or Molly Stark sleeps a widow."

Toward sunset, Baum called off his men, himself mortally wounded. Half of his 1,500 troops lay dead or wounded and the living were prisoners, surrounded by Stark's troops. Stark lost about two hundred men. Fortunately, as his weary men began to care for the wounded, Seth Warner arrived with his troop of Green Mountain Boys. These fresh men took over the camp duties and guard of the prisoners.

The New England troops rested several days, then joined the Continental troops at Saratoga, New York, where General Gates and 20,000 men stopped the advance of Burgoyne.

On August 26, 1777, a battle raged for two days that ended with the surrender of Burgoyne's British Army to the Continentals.

When Burgoyne realized the defeat was near, he looked, in vain, for reinforcements from the 1,500 soldiers whom he sent into New England, but of course they never returned and the battle was lost.

The defeat at Saratoga indicated the sound judgment of John Stark and the Continental Congress realized its unjust dishonor to this patriot. The Congress made Stark a brigadier general.

Four cannons were captured from the British at Bennington. Two of them were given to the Massachusetts troops. Their whereabouts are unknown. One of the other two is called "the Molly Stark Cannon" and is at New Boston.

The fourth cannon is at Plymouth, now in the custody of the American Legion. It is a French relic of the Battle of Quebec, bearing the name of the king of France. This cannon was brought to Plymouth about 1850 by the division superintendent of the Boston and Montreal Railroad, who was a former resident at New Boston.

END OF HOSTILITIES

After the close of the One Hundred Years' War, England claimed to be the "mistress of the sea" and was proud of her navy. In comparison with the American frigates that guarded the harbors from pirates, the hulls of the British ships were clumsy to handle and their rigging was not as well constructed.

During the Revolution at least one hundred British men-of-war sailed along the coast or lay in the harbors of the Americans, yet no blockade developed, perhaps because foreign trade almost ceased.

However, there was constant warfare against British shipping by American privateers. It was estimated that during the eight years of the Revolution, 30,000 seamen on American privateers engaged in this dangerous yet profitable business.

With the approval of the Continental Congress, American privateers sailed along the coast of England to capture trading vessels, then compelled them to sail to Spain where both ships and cargoes found a ready market. Scores of sea-captains became wealthy and their crews were also well paid.

The colonies did not possess a navy as such, but several of them individually owned vessels, just as New Hampshire built the *Raleigh* to attack British shipping. In time, twenty-one such vessels sailed the sea. The congress appointed a Maritime Committee to appoint their commander. Although but one of these ships remained afloat after the war, all of them destroyed many British ships and took many prizes.

In his book, *Ports of Piscataqua*, the statement is made by William G. Saltonstall that one of the chief reasons for the defeat of England in the Revolution was her inability to renew the masts of her navy. During the past years the forests of New Hampshire supplied the tall trees. Hundreds of these masts were shattered by the wind during the war which deprived the British both of vessels for their navy and ships to supply ammunition and provisions for their army.

New Hampshire produced its food and clothing and great was the satisfaction when a privateer brought a British supply ship into Portsmouth. The same pleasure prevailed when a boat loaded with cannon, muskets, and tons of ammunition was captured as it approached the coast of Maryland.

After 1777, New England was free from battlefields but thousands of men were enlisting to fill the twelve regiments from New Hampshire. The records on the military war rolls list 18,289 men. Many volunteers who enlisted for three months to a year, were honorably discharged to return to their homes and care for their farms. As the war dragged on, many soldiers reenlisted and the record of individuals is 12,479 from New Hampshire, which is a remarkable showing from a population of 82,000 inhabitants.

When requested for its quota of beef, New Hampshire furnished 1,500,000 pounds to the army and tons of potash for gunpowder. This was also remarkable because in varying sections of the state lack of rainfall and early frosts caused hunger both for humans and cattle. In 1778 and 1779, with only paper money for trade, at Portsmouth corn was priced at sixty dollars per bushel and hay was a thousand dollars a ton.

After the close of the war the French fleet that had served as a most valuable ally, sailed into Portsmouth for repairs in the shipyards. Sound money became plentiful again along the coast.

Lord Cornwallis was the last British general in the field. His army was surrounded at Yorktown in Virginia and he was obliged to surrender on October 19, 1781, and the Revolution was over. As always, months of negotiations followed before the Treaty of Peace was signed between Great Britain and the colonies on September 3, 1783.

Immediately, shipping became busy along the coast and in 1784 foreign goods began to appear in the markets "at reasonable prices" to quote Samuel Lane's diary.

JOHN PAUL JONES

The name of John Paul Jones is remembered in Portsmouth because the gambrel-roof house on Court Street is known as the John Paul Jones House of 1731. The Historical Society now occupies this famous colonial residence where a visitor may enjoy the priceless furnishing of the rooms.

John Paul was born at Aubrigland, Scotland, on July 6, 1747, the son of the gardener on the estate of William Craik beside the Solway Firth that almost divides Scotland from England.

The beautiful garden did not attract the lad. His favorite

sport was to stand upon the cliff and shout orders to the crew of an imaginary vessel. At the age of thirteen he was apprenticed for seven years to a merchant who traded in Barbados for rum, molasses, and sugar and in Virginia for tobacco.

After four years the merchant died and young Paul was free to be a sailor on ships that traded between England and the colonies. He was determined to become a captain, acquire a fortune, become the owner of an estate in Virginia where he would retire with a bride, and live the life of a gentleman in the atmosphere of *liberty*.

At twenty-one he was captain of a merchant ship, well-trained in navigation and the ability to trade a cargo on both sides of the sea. He read Shakespeare and the literature of his day. He gained the title of a "dandy skipper" with the appearance of a gentleman, in dress, manners, and language.

In 1770 he was admitted to the St. Bernardbe's Lodge of Masons in Kirkeudbright, Scotland, an honor for Captain John Paul of the brig *John*.

In this same year while on a long voyage, he ordered that a disobedient sailor be punished by "the cat" which was a whip with several lashes that were tipped with metal points. Later the sailor died of fever and his father believed that this whipping caused his son's death. When the ship arrived in port, Captain John Paul was arrested but the judge dismissed the accusation.

However, this incident caused John Paul to go to Philadelphia where he became involved in the plans for a Continental navy. Just as New Hampshire's Provincial Congress built the ship *Raleigh*, other colonies launched twenty-nine frigates and a marine committee of the Continental Congress appointed their commanders. Among them was Captain John Paul Jones.

Because of his unfortunate reputation, John Paul added the name Jones to his signature and he enlisted in the colonial navy as Captain John Paul Jones.

On June 14, 1777, a resolution passed in the Continental

Congress, "Resolved that the Flag of the United States be thirteen stripes alternate red and white, that the union be thirteen stars white in a blue field representing a new nation." Flag Day is June 14, annually, today.

On this same date, John Paul Jones was appointed to command a ship which was being built at the shipyard of John Langdon on Badger's Island in Portsmouth to be named *Ranger* in honor of Rogers' Rangers.

The handsome, thirty-year-old Captain Jones arrived in Portsmouth in 1777 where he was soon received by the social set, especially the ladies.

The young ladies of Portsmouth presented a flag for the *Ranger* sewed from silk of their dresses, the white being of a wedding gown. The French fleet exchanged a salute of nine guns to the *Ranger's* thirteen, the first honor to the Stars and Stripes when the *Ranger* joined with the French ships after France joined with the colonies in the Revolution.

Within the next two years Commander Jones won victories and prizes. The greatest victory was the battle of the *Bonhomme Richard* against the English warship *Serapis*. He returned to Philadelphia a famous hero.

Again he was sent to Portsmouth in 1779 to equip the *America* at John Langdon's shipyard. He boarded at the John Paul Jones House and enjoyed the friendship of St. John's Lodge No. 1, of the Masonic Order. Because of delays caused by the close of the Revolution, the *America* was not accepted but was given to the French fleet.

Commander Jones was troubled by disputes about prize money for his crews and he returned to France, never to see the colonies again.

For a period he served the rising nation of Russia, but a serious illness caused him to live in Paris where he died, forgotten, on July 18, 1792. A close friend took charge of his burial in a small cemetery in Paris, making certain that his body was embalmed and the grave site recorded.

In 1906 President Theodore Roosevelt began to search for the grave of Captain Jones which was fortunately discovered. A cruiser brought the body to Chesapeake Bay where it was met by four battleships and escorted to the Annapolis Naval Academy. Today the body of John Paul Jones rests within a marble sarcophagus. Thus America honors the patriot of liberty who is known as the founder of the American navy.

In Portsmouth in 1906 the Masonic Lodges, St. John's and St. Andrew's, conducted a Lodge of Sorrow in honor of Brother Jones with Dr. Ernest L. Silver speaking of "John Paul Jones, a patriot." Worshipful Master Edwin H. Adams spoke of "John Paul Jones, a Mason." Thus did New Hampshire honor a former resident after 129 years.

THE PATRIOT DOCTOR

Josiah Bartlett received an excellent inheritance from his English ancestors. His great-grandfather, Richard Bartlett, arrived in Newbury, Massachusetts, in 1636. His son Richard, born in 1648, had two sons, Joseph and Stephen.

Joseph became a doctor in Newton, New Hampshire. Stephen settled in Amesbury, Massachusetts. He married Hannah Webster on December 18, 1712. Four sons were born to this couple, Josiah being the fourth, born on November 21, 1729.

Josiah became a brilliant student. At the age of sixteen he began to study medicine with Dr. Nehemiah Ordway in Amesbury. Dr. Ordway's mother was a sister of Stephen Bartlett, Josiah's father.

Usually a student required seven years to complete his education, but Josiah became a doctor in five years.

He went to Kingston, New Hampshire, in 1750 at the age of twenty-one and lived in the home of Reverend Thomas Secombe who possessed a large and valuable library. In 1754 he married his cousin Mary, the daughter of his uncle, Joseph Bartlett of Newton.

Young Dr. Bartlett was willing to experiment. At this time

patients who were ill with fever were not given anything to relieve their thirst. When Josiah became ill with a high fever he demanded a quart of cider which he slowly drank throughout the night. In the morning his fever broke.

Another disease, known as "the throat distemper," became epidemic in Kingston. Instead of the usual treatment, Dr. Bartlett used Peruvian bark with marked success.

His outstanding contribution to medicine in New Hampshire was in 1791 when he wrote the charter for the New Hampshire Medical Society and became its first president. Dartmouth College had already conferred the honorary degree of doctor of medicine in 1790.

During the busy practice of his profession, Dr. Bartlett found time to participate in public life. In 1765, the year of the hated Stamp Act, he was elected to the Provincial Assembly.

In 1767 Governor John Wentworth appointed him a justice of the peace, then an important office, and later a colonel of militia.

Josiah Bartlett remained on the patriot side as the controversy increased between King George III and the colony. He was appointed to the Committee of Correspondence of the Assembly and later a member of the first Provincial Congress that met at Exeter. This congress elected him to the First Continental Congress, but he was obliged to refuse because his home in Kingston was burned by Tories and he was rebuilding the house for his growing family.

In the summer of 1775 he was elected to the Second Continental Congress. How he traveled to Philadelphia is not on record, whether by coasting schooner or on horseback, a journey of about a week. He was reelected in 1776 and gave the first vote on July 2 in support of the Declaration of Independence.

Worn out, he declined reelection in 1777. Yet he joined General John Stark that summer at the Battle of Bennington where he was wounded. In 1778 and 1779 he was back in the Continental Congress and voted for the Articles of Confederation, the first American constitution.

Returning to New Hampshire in 1779, he was appointed a justice of the superior court and chief justice in 1788.

In 1790 he was elected president of the state of New Hampshire and reelected in 1791 and again in 1792 when he carried nearly three-fourths of the votes in the state. The name president was changed to governor in June, 1793.

In January of 1794 he retired to private life. He died in the spring of 1795 at the age of sixty-six.

Of his family of twelve children, his three sons became doctors: Levi in Haverhill, Josiah, Jr., in Kingston, and Ezra in Warner. Four of Ezra's sons became doctors and also a son of Levi's.

Amesbury has always been proud of being the birthplace of the second signer of the Declaration of Independence. A bronze and granite monument of Josiah Bartlett stands at the head of Main Street in the city, the gift of Jacob R. Huntoon, pioneer carriage manufacturer of Amesbury. On the fourth of July, 1888, the monument was unveiled before a crowd of dignitaries of the state, thousands of citizens, and numerous descendants of the Bartlett family. A poem, "One of the Signers" by John Greenleaf Whittier was read on this occasion.

The Bartlett house is there in Kingston today with the linden tree that grew from a twig that Dr. Bartlett brought in his pocket from Philadelphia.

MESHECH WEARE

The old idea that parents searched the Bible to select names for their sons seems to be proved when Nathaniel Weare found Meshech with Daniel in the lion's den.

Meshech Weare was born on June 16, 1713, at Hampton Falls. As was true for many boys of the time who earned a brilliant record in public school, Meshech was selected for college and graduated at Harvard in 1735 and prepared for the ministry.

He became a successful preacher but his town chose him for public offices of selectman, justice of the peace, and colonel of the military. He represented Hampton in the Provincial Assembly in 1752 and in 1754 he was sent to Albany to assist in making a treaty of peace with the "Six Nations," the Iroquois tribes who were allies with England.

When Governor John Wentworth dissolved the Provincial Assembly, Meshech Weare was a delegate from Hampton to the Provincial Congress, which was the controlling government for New Hampshire from 1775 to 1784. He voted on December 21, 1775 that New Hampshire separate from England. With the advice of the Continental Congress, New Hampshire became a state and adopted a constitution.

This constitution provided for a House of Representatives and a Council (Senate) but no Executive. This power was placed in a Committee of Safety consisting of eight or more members of the Congress. Meshech Weare was elected president of this committee because of his reputation for "moderation, intelligence, and honesty." Later the name of president was changed to governor.

President Weare was a busy official. When the Provincial Congress was in session, he was chairman of the Council and in 1776 was appointed chief justice of the Superior Court. Fortunately his home in Hampton Falls was but an hour's ride to Exeter where the Congress met.

The Committee of Safety supervised the collection of the state tax which paid the soldiers in the regiments. The Congress authorized borrowing money and printing of paper money, raised several regiments of enlisted men, and appointed their officers. Law and order were enforced throughout the state.

The Continental Congress assigned quotas for beef and rum annually to every state. New Hampshire filled its quota for beef but only about half of the rum. This was imported from the West Indies Islands. The interior towns were not able to provide the demand.

Little can be realized today of the hardships that New Hampshire suffered throughout the years of the American

Revolution. The harbor of Portsmouth was closed by the English and all trade was stopped. The result was that every family was obliged to raise its own food and clothes or find the means to buy them. Money was not available and barter became necessary, especially after paper money became almost worthless.

Inflation increased rapidly. Early frosts, army worms, and severe drought, with forest fires caused the crops to be reduced and corn became scarce even in the inland towns. The worthless paper money was refused by farmers.

In the year 1779 corn was $15 per bushel, rum was $21 per gallon, molasses $15 per gallon, and sugar $12 per barrel. These were fixed prices by the state, but as food became more difficult to buy, hungry people paid $30 or $40 per bushel and $2 per pound for beef. Hay was $50 per ton. Rum became $660 per gallon but cider was plentiful and was $20 per barrel.

The loyalists or Tories were doing everything in their power to disturb the state. They made counterfeit money. They published untrue information.

About twenty-five leaders in the patriot cause were trusted, honest officials. John Sullivan was called the right hand of George Washington, John Langdon used his wealth to finance the Battle of Bennington and fought there. Neither of the two men served upon the Committee of Safety.

Sixteen men were named on this committee, scattered from Orford to Durham. From 1775 to 1777 the committee sat during the time that the legislature was not in session, but between 1778 and 1784 it was in continuous session.

The legislature elected them to the committee and expected them to execute its policies. A prominent Tory said, "New Hampshire had never a more energetic government, nor a more honest one."

When the new Constitution of 1784 was adopted, and the Committee of Safety was abolished, Meshech Weare was elected state president but he declined the office because of

ill health. He retired to his home in Hampton Falls. He died
in 1786 leaving a reputation that few could equal.

NEW HAMPSHIRE LOYALISTS

Looking backward through two hundred years reveals the
pattern of the American Revolution. In 1770 three regiments
of British soldiers were quartered at Boston to control the
Sons of Liberty.

The Boston Massacre began the fighting on March 5,
1770. Groups of militia were soon training in the towns of
New Hampshire.

At this time the population of New Hampshire numbered
82,000, consisting of two political parties: loyalists and
patriots, and a third group concerned with neither party.

The loyalists, around thirty thousand people, believed in
the British government. Their ancestors were English. They
wished to remain Englishmen. The majority of them did not
participate in the Revolution. However, only one hundred
families of loyalists were banished from the state.

Governor John Wentworth used his influence to persuade
the colony to remain loyal to the king. In Portsmouth and
along the seacoast many loyalists were the wealthy shipbuilders and merchants who were enjoying comfortable
daily life in their beautiful homes.

The loyalist party was unorganized, although as Governor
Wentworth began to become unpopular, sixty-six of his
friends united to assist him.

The active loyalists were called Tories meaning traitors
by the patriots who organized a military company in Portsmouth with a sea captain, Thomas Pickering, its leader. At
least 400 men were ready to respond to the beat of a drum
should mob violence arise in the town.

What might be called a "hostility gap" today began between the loyalists and all other inhabitants. The situation
became so dangerous that Governor Wentworth appealed to

General Gage in Boston for two hundred British soldiers. These men were not allowed, but first a small frigate and then the warship *Scarborough* were anchored in the harbor with provisions for a week.

Meanwhile Governor Wentworth fled to Fort William and Mary with his family. When the food supply for the *Scarborough* needed to be replenished, nothing could be purchased in Portsmouth and the commander decided to return to Boston.

Governor Wentworth sailed with the ship, never to return. He soon fled to England, a disheartened loyalist.

Both parties believed in their cause. The loyalists were wealthy, influential, and arrogant. They used dishonest means to overcome their opponents. They spread false rumors, spied upon the patriots, counterfeited money, and served in large numbers in the British Army. They were unorganized and outnumbered.

Committees of Safety were formed by the patriots in every town. When a loyalist became too disagreeable, he might be confined in an unsanitary prison for an indefinite term or be tried and compelled to sign an apology and agree to refrain from further unpopular actions.

After the legislature declared the independence of the colony from England in December, 1775, the Committee of Safety of the Provincial Congress made a law that loyalists were allowed three months to sell their property and leave the state.

Twenty-five wealthy families of Portsmouth fled either to Canada, Nova Scotia, or Long Island where the British were in control.

In 1778 a law was enacted that the property of the loyalists be confiscated and sold to increase the treasury of the patriots. Not a large amount was realized because too many agents were necessary to prove deeds and complete the transactions.

These refugees were forbidden to return to New Hampshire. A few attempted to disobey this law but were banished and threatened with death if they appeared again. Although Governor Wentworth became governor of Nova Scotia and lived there until 1820, he did not dare to visit his native state, but his wife and son were allowed, in later years, to visit relatives in Portsmouth.

In March of 1776 the Continental Congress recommended to the colonies that all persons who opposed the Revolution be disarmed. To determine who these persons were an association test was recommended. On April 12, 1776, the Committee of Safety sent such a test to all of the towns in New Hampshire. All who signed promised to support the Revolution to the utmost of their ability, even to bearing arms. All who refused to sign, except conscientious objectors, were labeled loyalists. Today signers are considered patriots and their descendants are eligible for membership in certain patriotic societies.

Most unjust was the persecution of members of the Episcopal Church in Portsmouth and especially in Claremont. They were beaten, drawn through mud and water; many were imprisoned, and others were confined to the limits of the town.

The loyalists expected that the British would win the war and they used every means to hinder the Revolution. The patriots were fighting for liberty and for their very lives. As we view the past, two hundred years later, we recall the old adage, "All is fair in love and war."

In 1795 nine towns were shown on the map of New Hampshire.

⟨5⟩
The Ninth State

THE THIRTEEN NATIONS

When the Treaty of Peace was signed with England, thirteen small nations occupied the coast of the Atlantic Ocean from Maine to Georgia and inland to the Appalachian Mountains.

They called themselves the United States, yet they were by no means united. From their first settlement certain conditions were taken for granted. A householder was considered a freeman in all of the colonies, and if a man committed a crime anywhere, he was a criminal everywhere. He could not flee to another colony to escape punishment.

Every colony possessed local customs, government, and laws. Now the small states feared that Virginia, Pennsylvania, New York, and Massachusetts would dominate the nation because of their population and wealth. States' rights were obstacles to union.

When the Declaration of Independence was declared by the Continental Congress, regardless of the number of delegates from a colony, there were thirteen votes and nine were necessary for an affirmative acceptance of any resolution. This congress possessed advisory powers only.

Land was the first problem to solve. Every colony with the exception of Maryland was claiming many square miles outside of its original grant. New Hampshire called Vermont "the New Hampshire Grants" (for Benning Wentworth had ventured to grant several townships in southern Vermont) while New York claimed the Champlain Valley and the Green Mountain Boys under Ethan Allen denied the claims of both colonies.

Georgia considered its territory extended to the Mississippi River, Virginia fought the French for the Northwest Territory in the Ohio Valley, and Massachusetts was invading the wilderness to the south of the Great Lakes.

Maryland insisted that all of these territories should belong to the United States and so this problem was finally settled.

Money did not exist, for British coins disappeared when trade ceased. Although the colonies issued paper money called scrip, it soon became about worthless without anything to redeem it except promises.

In Portsmouth, while hay and corn were scarce, a ton of hay was valued at 1,000 paper dollars. Trade was by barter everywhere.

Voting privileges differed from colony to colony. In the beginning, New Hampshire permitted a vote to the head of a family in town meetings. Some colonies required that a voter own land, while others demanded a certain amount of money. New Jersey, for a time, allowed women to vote if they possessed property.

After the war all states, with the exception of Rhode Island and Connecticut, compiled new constitutions. In New Hampshire, only the payment of a poll tax by a male was necessary for him to vote and this same situation prevailed in several other states.

The problems increased in number between 1783 and 1787. Finally, the Continental Congress called upon the states to send delegates to a convention that would meet in Philadelphia with instructions to "amend" the Articles of Confederation to form a Union.

These fifty-two delegates met on May 18, 1787, with George Washington the presiding officer. Immediately they closed the doors and all promised that everything that transpired should remain a secret. These men kept their agreement for four months.

The delegates were mostly men who possessed property. They were honest, intelligent patriots who expressed their ideas in long speeches and debated wisely. A few delegates returned to their homes. Late in September 1787, the doors were opened and an entirely new Constitution appeared while the Articles of Confederation were scrapped.

Scholars declare that the Constitution of the United States is one of the most remarkable documents of its nature ever written. With the exception of its Bill of Rights, only sixteen other amendments have been adopted and one of these was repealed.

The next and very difficult task was to persuade the states to ratify this new Constitution. Each state would have a vote and nine states voting in the affirmative would make the document operative.

The small states were not convinced that the rights of the individual citizens were assured. Rhode Island did not ratify the Constitution before the nation was established, yet became a part of the Union.

Virginia and New York, the most populous states, held aloof until they were really compelled to unite, when nine states ratified in 1788.

THE STATE
RATIFIES THE CONSTITUTION

Between September and December, 1787, eight states ratified the proposed Constitution for the United States. New Hampshire delayed. Not until December was a convention of delegates assembled at Exeter to debate ratification. This debate continued into February, 1788.

New Hampshire was one of the small states that feared lest its citizens would be of little influence in the nation. Before consenting to ratification, the people desired to establish the right of every individual to freedom with liberty and justice for all.

Perhaps the delegate with the greatest legal experience was Samuel Livermore of Holderness, the former advisor to Governor Benning Wentworth in the Admiralty Court and to Governor John Wentworth as king's attorney.

As he perceived the trend of the convention, he concluded that to risk a motion to ratify was unwise at the start of the debate. He believed in ratification and did not desire a negative vote.

He made a motion to adjourn the convention until June, to meet at Concord, the town that had been selected for the capitol of the new state. Everybody seemed ready to go home and the motion carried.

Mid-February was a cold season for a horseback ride to all sections of New Hampshire. Samuel Livermore and the three delegates from his vicinity of Holderness must have traveled through snow over one hundred fifty miles of bridle paths, whether they chose the Coos Road over the hills of Gilmanton, the Governor's Road to Wolfeborough and the Dartmouth College Road, or across the state to the Merrimack River and then northward to Holderness.

It may be wise to reflect about the hardships that our ancestors endured while establishing the United States: war, long journeys on foot or horseback, absence from home and family, and far more.

Living across the Pemigewasset River from Holderness was another delegate who favored ratification, Francis Worcester. He was highly respected and a deacon in the town of Plymouth.

The story about to be told is history in Holderness. Samuel Livermore and Francis Worcester had plans when the convention adjourned. They knew which delegates favored ratification, those who were undecided, and those who were definitely opposed.

During the weeks between March and June these two delegates mounted their horses to ride to visit many delegates with the hope that each of them would vote for ratification in June.

Samuel Livermore delivered an eloquent address before the one hundred four delegates who gathered within the meeting at the "Northend" in Concord in June, 1788. The vote was taken. Fifty-seven delegates voted for ratification and forty-seven against. This was far from a unanimous convention.

But there was one if in this affirmative vote. As in several other states, New Hampshire's approval rested with the provision that the first session of the Congress of the United States offer a Bill of Rights to amend the Constitution, ratifying freedom of religion, speech, assembly, press, and petition. Also, what has been known since the old Saxon days as *the Right of Castle*—no man's home can be searched without a definite search warrant. The right of a fair and just trial by jury is assured.

Papers were immediately prepared to report this vote and a rider was told to spare neither himself nor horses to race to New York with the expectation that New Hampshire would be the ninth state to ratify and make possible the United States as a nation.

Four other states had not ratified at this time but Virginia was assembled in convention. The rider from New Hampshire arrived before the affirmative vote of Virginia was reported.

With rapidity candidates were elected for president, vice-president, and for Congress. George Washington received the greatest number of votes for president, John Adams for vice-president.

The Congress met in New York and John Langdon of New Hampshire was elected president of the Senate, pro tem. The inauguration ceremonies were held in New York on June 30, 1789, when John Langdon had the honor to administer the oath that confirmed George Washington as president of the United States. The nation was established.

GENERAL WASHINGTON
VISITS PORTSMOUTH

"First in War, first in Peace, first in the Hearts of his Countrymen."

If proof of these words were required, the reason that he expressed for his visit to the small town of Portsmouth would be one answer. He said that he wished to call upon the mother of his private secretary, Tobias Lear.

This young man was the fifth in his family to bear the name of Tobias. He was born on September 19, 1760, in a hip-roofed house on Hunkin Street in Portsmouth that his grandfather erected in 1740.

His father was a wealthy shipmaster and landowner who sent his son to Harvard College where he graduated in 1783 and then traveled the following year in Europe.

When President Washington was looking for a private secretary, he asked the advice of his former officer, General Lincoln, who recommended young Lear as did a clergyman of Boston.

During the following sixteen years, until the death of Washington, he filled the position of secretary and also was the tutor for the two adopted children of the president, and managed many financial affairs of the estate of Mount Vernon in Virginia. He lived with the family and became like a foster son and the personal confidant of the president.

Soon after his inauguration Washington began to visit the states and was in Massachusetts in October, 1789, accompanied by Tobias Lear. On October 29 with a small military escort they started toward Portsmouth, remaining overnight in Newburyport.

The following morning the party rode up along the bank of the Merrimack River to the ferry to Amesbury where the first bridge over the river was built three years later. No doubt the saddles were carried in the ferry boat while the horses were swimming the river.

On Rocky Hill above the river a new meetinghouse was standing where a company of veterans from Amesbury and Salisbury had gathered to welcome their beloved general.

Standing upon the steps of the front porch, Washington spoke cordial words of greeting and expressed his admiration for the services these soldiers had rendered.

When the party entered New Hampshire, Governor John Sullivan and John Langdon with their officials of the state and a troop of cavalry were waiting to escort them into Portsmouth where the streets were crowded by citizens from the surrounding countryside.

Thirteen cannons boomed, the three church bells were ringing, one of them from the capture of Louisburg in 1748, the fifes and drums were playing, and shouts of welcome filled the air.

From the balcony above the front door of the State House, President Washington addressed the multitude although few were able to hear his words. He made a fine appearance dressed in his buff and blue uniform, short trousers, white silk hose, low shoes with silver buckles, and his three-cornered hat. After his long ride, he was escorted to the tavern to rest for the night.

On Sunday he attended the morning service at Queen's Chapel, accompanied by Theodore Atkinson, secretary of state in New Hampshire. They occupied the Governor's Pew. This was a platform, raised two steps above the main floor, covered by a red carpet. Above was a canopy draped with dark red velvet and furnished with the two hand-carved chairs upholstered in red damask, the gifts of Queen Catherine.

Without doubt the rector, Reverend Arthur Brown, displayed the heavy silk, royal purple vestment and the other of cloth of gold, also gifts of Queen Catherine, and used the silver communion set during the service.

In the afternoon the president listened to the long sermon by the Puritan clergyman in the meetinghouse that seated many of the citizens.

On Monday a sail down the river to Fort William and Mary permitted the president to view the dangerous entrance to the harbor. Perhaps as a result he soon began to establish a lighthouse at Portland.

Governor John Sullivan entertained with a banquet on Tuesday and Senator John Langdon held a reception in his new mansion on Pleasant Street which the president described later as the most beautiful Georgian house he had seen.

The last day of his visit was given to Washington's call upon Mrs. Lear and her daughter. Thursday morning Washington started the return journey to Boston.

To appreciate the effort this visit demanded, reflect how today we ride at seventy miles per hour in comfortably upholstered machines on land and fly at terrific speeds. Try then, to imagine what traveling over six hundred miles from Virginia to Portsmouth in the saddle at the rate of a mile in ten minutes would be like. George Washington lived years upon horseback both in war and in peace.

After Washington's death, Tobias Lear became a diplomat in the West Indies and in the Barbary States. Later he was employed in the Treasury Department in Washington where he suddenly died. He sleeps in "The Point of Graves Cemetery" that is found near the bank of the river at Portsmouth south of Strawbery Banke. This ancient graveyard was fenced by Thomas Pickering in 1672 for a "burying ground forever," and he, only, had "liberty to pasture his neat cattle" there.

THREE ECONOMIC DEVELOPMENTS

Early in the nineteenth century three factors influenced the economy of New Hampshire. The first was the discovery of the Old Man of the Mountain. Three workmen who were building a road between Franconia and Plymouth claimed this honor in 1805.

Luke Brooks knelt to wash his hands in Profile Lake. As he arose his gaze caught the stone face. Astonished, he called to his companion, Francis Whitcomb, to verify the sight.

The third discoverer was Nathaniel Hall of Thornton who left the camp to hunt for a partridge for his breakfast. He saw the face and summoned all the occupants of the camp to view this sight.

The first road into Thornton and Woodstock began at Moultonboro and extended through Sandwich Notch and along the east side of the Pemigewasset River.

A family named Gurnsey had built their cabin in 1807 on the present site of the Indian Head Motel. Probably hunting was their aim. A ninety-three-year-old Aunt Jess wandered along the brooks to enjoy her hobby of fishing. One day she returned to the cabin greatly excited about a beautiful brook that she discovered. She finally prevailed upon a member of the family to accompany her to this wonderful spot.

Thus the Flume was found with its waterfall and the hanging boulder that was wedged between the high granite walls about half the distance between the brook and the top of the chasm.

Fortunately Benjamin W. Kilburn of Littleton traveled about with his camera on his shoulder or this enormous hanging boulder would be only a myth today, because on June 30, 1883, a terrific tempest flooded the Flume causing the boulder, weighing tons, to crash, probably into many fragments. No trace of it has been discovered. Several of the Kilburn stereoscopic views of this hanging rock are preserved by families in Littleton verifying the fact that glaciers left this boulder in its precarious position and its loss is to be regretted.

After Governor Benning Wentworth granted the towns of Lisbon, Littleton, Landaff, and Franconia in 1763, settlers followed the trail up the Connecticut Valley and along the Ammonoosuc River.

The second event was the discovery of a vein of iron at Franconia in 1790, two and a half feet wide, ten miles long, beneath the surface of Iron Mountain.

A small foundry opened in 1802 on the bank of Gale River near the present bridge on the road to Sugar Hill, called the Lower Works. The state geologist assayed the vein at ninety-six percent high grade iron, some titanium and flint.

Another greater vein was discovered on Ore Hill in 1805. A second foundry began two miles south called the Upper Works that became the Franconia and Haverhill Company and the Lower Works was named the New Hampshire Iron Factory Company.

In 1810 the Lower Works was taken over by a group of businessmen from southern New Hampshire who sunk shafts deeply into Ore Hill and added many buildings. Both companies began to produce wrought iron used for farm tools, carriage irons, andirons, sledges, and chains.

Next the famous Franconia stoves replaced the kitchen fireplaces and both round and box designs were in the living rooms in this region.

Although this seems unbelievable, after 1838 Franconia was the iron center of the United States. The small village supported eleven saloons. The streets were so covered with soot that the children walked to school through the fields.

Business was at its peak. It produced 750,000 pounds of iron at two cents per pound and 200,000 pounds of cast iron at four cents per pound. Railroads were not yet running in this region and transportation was by horse drawn wagons.

The third event was the introduction of cotton mills into the state. The first mill was erected in New Ipswich in 1804. Samuel Blodgett of Manchester completed the upper canal in 1807 which controlled the power of Amoskeag Falls. The first cotton mill in Manchester was established in 1810.

So rapidly did this business increase that by 1823 there were twenty-eight cotton mills and eighteen woolen mills in New Hampshire using the water power of the Merrimack River to run their looms. The Amoskeag cotton mill began operation in 1819.

Many young women from the farms came to work in these mills at wages of less than a dollar per day. The companies erected dormitories and opened dining rooms at reasonable prices that left a profit for these girls at the end of the week. Each operator attended five or six looms..

THE GRANITE STATE
AND THE WAR OF 1812

Seldom do we recall that on June 18, 1812, the Congress of the United States declared war upon the Mother Country for a second time. Since the former treaty of peace, England had claimed the power of "Mistress of the Sea" and her arbitrary demands were the cause of this second war. Once again she demanded that all foreign trade of our country be from her ports and nothing should be bought from her enemy, France.

At that time two political parties were becoming active; the Federalist which sympathized with England and the Republican which demanded freedom of trade for the Republic. The New England states were largely Federalists, they even talked of secession. But the younger element influenced for war.

When our country refused to obey the demands of England as early as 1803, she began to capture our ships and to impress their crews. Before 1812, 900 American vessels had been captured and 10,000 sailors impressed, according to the records of reliable historians.

England was proud of her navy of approximately one thousand men-of-war that she was using to blockade harbors and to protect her shipping. The United States possessed three frigates: the *Constitution, President,* and *United States,* all superior to the British. Also, there were about twenty armed sloops manned by crews of Marines who guarded our harbors from pirates.

But, just as in the Revolution, privateers preyed upon British ships. During the war 3,000 prizes were taken. Even English sea captains connived with the Americans for a share in this booty.

England immediately blockaded our harbors and sent troops to Canada because our Congress had ambitions to annex that country. The Canadians were loyal to England and by December, 1812, they had captured Detroit and Fort Dearborn (now Chicago).

The English intended to invade New York but were checked at the Battle of Lake Erie on September 10, 1813, where Admiral Perry's dying words were "Don't give up the ship."

Again another defeat prevented this plan when the battle on Lake Champlain at Plattsburg was won by Commodore MacDonough.

In August, 1814, the British sent a fleet up the Chesapeake Bay and landed 4,500 troops who fought a battle at Blandsburg, Maryland, and then marched upon Washington. President Madison and his officials fled to Virginia and his famous wife, Dolly Madison, gathered up the silver spoons and fled to safety.

The "Palace"—as the home of the president was called—was gutted and many public buildings were burned, yet the population of the city was not harmed. Next, Baltimore was attacked. Its protecting Fort McHenry stood firm and the battle failed. This was the scene of "The Star Spangled Banner," by Francis Scott Key.

After two months, the troops sailed for New Orleans, intending to block the Mississippi River. Here they were met by Andrew Jackson, known as "Old Rough and Ready," for he was a backwoodsman and his 5,000 troops were the same. When he looked over the situation, he knew that his army must fight behind some protection. He chose a swamp and erected a high barricade. Depending upon their bayonets, the British, 10,000 strong, advanced in line and were cut down like ripe grain. Again they advanced and the same happened. The British lost 1,914 men on that January day.

Over in Holland at Ghent a treaty of peace had been arranged two weeks before the Battle of New Orleans, but it was not ratified by Congress. This successful engagement really finished the war. This settled the question of the trade relations of our country.

New Hampshire feared invasion during these three years because British war vessels lay around Portsmouth, but Fort William and Mary protected the harbor. The town of Rye armed for a possible attack with two cannon on the green and General Goss drilled a company and armed his men with guns and ammunition. A supply of powder and balls was stored beneath the roof of the meetinghouse.

On May 29, 1814, terror spread when two British men-of-war anchored off a reef several miles from shore (now named Gunboat Shoals). A schooner sailed by and a barge from the warship followed it toward Rye harbor.

Two boys were sent to ask that one of the cannon be brought from Rye. Immediately horses were attached to the cannon and began to run at full speed down the hill. Suddenly the bottom fell from the powder box. Then one horse balked—with the result that the cannon did not arrive at the harbor, but the boys returned in time to watch the fight.

When the schooner entered the harbor the barge followed. General Goss had divided his company to place his men on both sides of the entrance. His order to fire was obeyed so rapidly that the supply of ammunition was soon gone.

It was believed that several British sailors were wounded. The barge immediately withdrew and the two warships sailed away before troops arrived from Portsmouth.

This brief alarm was the only gunfire upon the soil of New Hampshire.

SLAVERY AND THE UNDERGROUND RAILROAD

Slavery is as old as civilization. The trade in Negro slaves captured in Africa was well established before the first shipload was sold in Jamestown, Virginia, in 1619.

Within the next century southern planters were buying slaves for their cotton and tobacco fields and as servants in their homes. Gradually the custom spread northward, especially for servants in wealthy families.

Probably Jonathan Warner was the first householder in New Hampshire to staff his home with Negro servants, although slaves were owned in Portsmouth much earlier. The wealthy shipbuilders began to purchase Negro butlers and trained southern cooks, Negro coachmen, and houseboys. In Portsmouth Negro slaves numbered one hundred sixty in 1754—sixty were women.

A law was enacted that every new town must open a house for the entertainment of strangers. The home of David Webster became a tavern at Plymouth and he purchased two slaves in 1764. Cisco and Dinah became servants in the family of ten boys and one daughter. They rest today in Trinity cemetery in Holderness near the grave of their master.

After the Grafton County court house was erected in 1774, another slave, named Jupiter, owned by the first store-keeper in Plymouth, was tried in court and convicted of stealing. He was sentenced to be publicly whipped on the following morning. Since no jail was available, the sheriff tied him to a large tree near the court house since the night was warm. A merciful person cut his bonds during the night to permit Jupiter to disappear, but his name was not forgotten while Jupiter's tree remained standing.

That one human being should have the right to own another rankled the New England conscience of the Puritans. Also the cold climate of Portsmouth was not conducive to the health of the southern Negro. In 1795 the Assembly of New Hampshire abolished slavery in the province.

When William Lloyd Garrison began to publish his anti-slavery newspaper, the *Liberator,* and gradually organized three hundred antislavery societies, he received cooperation in New Hampshire.

An active movement began in Concord that published a newspaper, the *Herald of Freedom.* The poet John Green-leaf Whittier came to Concord to assist in promoting the movement and aroused such resentment that he, with others, were obliged to seek police protection.

The Underground Railroad developed many stations in New Hampshire to assist runaway slaves to escape to Canada. One trail operated through Concord to Plymouth.

When the fine home of Theodore Peabody Rogers that stood on Main Street in Concord was demolished, a secret closet was discovered with a sliding wall where slaves had been hidden. Another large house in Woodstock was the next station. The large brick chimney was found to conceal a secret place at the height of the second floor.

Today the claim is made that the lower section of Polar Caves called Smugglers' Pass and a connecting cave were other hiding places for a night.

DANIEL WEBSTER
IN THE GRANITE STATE

Daniel Webster, who died in 1852, is considered by many to be the greatest stateman and orator in the history of our country. His purpose was to prevent the spread of slavery outside of the southern states.

Ebenezer Webster, the father of Daniel, was an honest, intelligent pioneer born in Kingston, New Hampshire, in 1739.

He lived with Ebenezer Stevens who removed to the present town of Salisbury, New Hampshire, in 1751. The boy never attended a public school yet he managed to learn to read. Soon he was one of Colonel Rogers' Rangers.

He married Mehitable Smith. They lost three of their five children before Mehitable died leaving a tiny baby Joseph. Soon Ebenezer married Abigail Eastman who cared for his two children and proved to be a wise mother to her own five offspring.

Ezekiel was born to this union in 1780, a strong youngster, but Daniel, born in 1782, was so weak that the neighbors who saw him believed that he would not survive. When his mother heard their opinion she resolved that they be proven wrong, so she cared for him so faithfully that at ten years of age he was rolling logs in his father's sawmill.

Ebenezer was appointed judge of the county court with a salary of $400. He resolved that Daniel should receive an education and took him to Phillips Exeter Academy in the spring of 1794 where he stayed nine months. His scholarship was excellent, yet the lad was not happy because the students laughed at his rural dress and habits.

The next year he studied Latin and Greek with Dr. Wood, the minister at Boscawen, and entered Dartmouth College in August of 1797. Entrance qualifications were not strict, for he knew no mathematics, geography, or history. He was excellent in Latin, read widely in literature and history, and was soon considered the best general student in the college. His ability in speaking was so eloquent that in

1800 the citizens of Hanover requested that he deliver their Fourth of July oration.

He graduated from Dartmouth in 1801 and, at his father's request, began to read law with the next door neighbor. A family decision that Ezekiel should receive a college education obliged Daniel to accept a teaching position in Fryeburg, Maine, for the following two years. He copied legal papers in the evenings to permit the entire salary to be given to Ezekiel.

Daniel hoped to study in a law office in Boston. This opportunity came when he was finding a teaching position for Ezekiel in a private school. There he met the outstanding lawyer in the city, Christopher Gore, who was so impressed by the young man that he offered him a position in his office where he remained until he passed the bar in Massachusetts in 1805.

A law office was immediately opened in Boscawen. He did not make his first plea in the courthouse in Plymouth, as is often claimed, but he did gain a reputation there when he spoke against capital punishment. He earned about $600 annually which was considered above the average in a small community.

In 1807 Ezekiel was admitted to the bar and Daniel permitted his brother to take over the office in Boscawen and he removed to Portsmouth where opportunities were larger and earnings increasing.

The following year he returned to Hopkinton, New Hampshire, to marry Grace Fletcher, the daughter of the minister. They resided in a two-story house on the corner of Court and Pleasant streets, where several children were born. They lived there until the great fire in 1813, then moved to High Street.

Politics drew Mr. Webster into the Federalist party and in 1813 he was elected to Congress from New Hampshire where he served for two years. While in Washington, he was admitted to practice before the United States Supreme Court in 1814.

Mr. Webster decided to remove to Boston in 1817 where

earnings from his practice immediately increased to $20,000 annually.

Daniel Webster gained fame when he pleaded the famous Dartmouth College case between the trustees of the college and the state in 1819 before the Supreme Court which preserved the charter of the college.

At the two hundredth anniversary of the landing of the Pilgrims at Plymouth, Mr. Webster delivered the oration that won for him great reknown. He was returned to Congress by Massachusetts and later sent to the Senate. At one time he was also a member of the president's cabinet.

He died in Marshfield, Massachusetts, on October 24, 1852.

THE WAR BETWEEN THE STATES

Although only a brief story about the Civil War can be told in this book, how New Hampshire fought to preserve the Union can at least be outlined.

The actual beginning was the result of the secession of South Carolina from the United States on December 20, 1860, just as that state declared its intention if Abraham Lincoln was elected president.

Soon Georgia, Alabama, Mississippi, Louisiana, and Florida followed and later Texas, Virginia, Arkansas, North Carolina, and Tennessee. A convention was held that elected Jefferson Davis president and a constitution was written.

Many causes are mentioned for this conflict such as the slavery issue and economic differences between the industrial North and the agricultural South revolving about the tariff question.

The first gun was fired upon Fort Sumter by the South on April 12, 1861. A ring of guns was placed toward the fort which stood in the harbor of Charleston, South Carolina. Surrender was demanded but Major Anderson had no order to lower the Stars and Stripes.

Food was gone and after two days of bombardment, Major Anderson marched his men out of the fort and the Southern general lowered the flag. No soldier was injured.

President Lincoln called for 375,000 enlistments, many for three months, because it was expected that the war would be of about a year's duration.

The army constituted about seventeen thousand soldiers, mostly stationed on the Western border. Many graduates of West Point were Southerners and these men enlisted in the South as did many of the army men.

The North had the advantage of twenty-two million while the South numbered only nine million, and about one-third of these were slaves.

The firearms were manufactured in the North but the South had stored war supplies, it was claimed, in anticipation of war. The South was fighting upon its own ground, thus less troops were required, since the North must guard the ground that they captured.

Foreign nations were sympathetic with the South because they needed the cotton for their industries. The Northern navy consisted of but thirty-one active ships, many of them scattered abroad. Until many more vessels could be found the Southern ports could not be blockaded.

When the news about Fort Sumter was known in the North, volunteers rapidly offered their services. The quota for New Hampshire was 780 men and 2,004 enlisted for three months.

The first regiment was completely equipped by the state and the banks subscribed $680,000. The regiment was mustered into service and left Concord on May 25 for Washington by train amidst the music of bands and waving of flags.

The men camped twelve days near Washington, then were ordered to cross the Potomac River to join an army that was marching to fight the "rebels." Before any action began, the general ordered his troops to retreat. By this time the three-month enlistment for this regiment was about to expire. The volunteers returned to Concord and were discharged; about half of them reenlisted in other regiments.

The second and third regiments volunteered for three years and were immediately ordered to guard along the seacoast from Charleston to Savannah. The troops were untrained and eighteen months were required before the really hard fighting began in 1862.

New Hampshire furnished seventeen regiments which included 32,750 soldiers. The exact number killed is unknown. Several regiments lost one third of their men in battles. Many more died of measles and smallpox in Southern prisons.

In addition to the eighteen volunteer regiments of infantry, New Hampshire sent three companies of riflemen, the First Volunteer Battery, the First Volunteer Cavalry, a battalion for the New England Cavalry, the First Regiment of Volunteer Heavy Artillery, and over one thousand men who served in the navy.

The battleship *Kearsarge* was built in the Navy Yard at Portsmouth with timbers that were cut on Mount Kearsarge in Warner. On June 19, 1864, the *Kearsarge* sank the Confederate vessel *Alabama* which in two years had taken sixty-two prizes upon the high seas.

Ulysses S. Grant was the final general of the Northern Army and Robert E. Lee was commander of the Confederate forces.

On Palm Sunday, April 9, 1865, Lee surrendered to Grant at Appomattox Court House in Virginia. By May 26, other forces surrendered and the war came to an end.

This is not a pleasant history story to relate about two sections of a nation so bitterly opposed that they fought four years. The seceding states returned to the United States but the memory of bitter strife lingers long after the 1865 ending of the war.

HOW WOMEN
SERVED IN THE CIVIL WAR

At the beginning of the Civil War women offered their services. As men enlisted, women filled their places as school teachers, factory workers, clerks in the offices of the government; they managed farms and plantations, and became nurses in military hospitals and on the battle fields.

Two public hospitals existed in 1861, the Bellevue in New York City and the Massachusetts General in Boston. Nurses were men. Sanitation was an unknown word.

Military surgeons protested when women insisted that they could imitate the example of Florence Nightingale, but to their surprise women possessed courage to serve in field hospitals and give first aid on the battle fields. Then doctors began to train nurses.

Groups of women met in churches to prepare uniforms, to cut their linen sheets and tablecloths for bandages, and scrape linen for lint to prepare for sponges in both the North and South.

Soldiers lived in tents and slept on cots if possible. Each man was furnished a knapsack for his personal effects and a blanket. Cleanliness was difficult with mosquitoes in swarms, lice, fleas, and germs. Measles, chicken pox and smallpox, malaria, and typhoid fever were a constant danger. Many more men died from disease than from wounds.

A battlefield can hardly be described—the roar and smoke of cannon, bang of guns, smell of powder, shrieks of wounded men and horses. First aid was given to the wounded men when possible. Field hospitals, where surgeons operated, were placed near the battlefields. Alcohol to the point of inebriation eased pain more or less.

Early in the war patriotic women organized relief societies in the large cities. The Hospital Aid Society of Spartanburg, South Carolina, and the Michigan Soldiers Relief Association in Washington were among the first. The Hebrew and the Philadelphia aid societies, and the Soldiers' Rest in Chicago, were ready, day or night, to serve soldiers, departing or returning. They fed thousands.

Three thousand wealthy women in New York City formed a Woman's Central Association whose aim was to look after the comfort of soldiers by supervising the training of nurses for military hospitals. This was the first of its kind in the United States. It opened on April 25, 1861.

It was the need to coordinate all of these services that led to the establishment, on June 9, 1861, of the United States Sanitary Commission in Chicago. Mrs. Mary A. Livermore and Mrs. Jane Hoge became co-chairmen with Reverend Henry W. Bellows as national president.

In 1861 the signature of a woman upon a bank check was not honored unless she possessed a personal account. Thus, necessity demanded that officers be men, although these women earned millions of dollars by commercial fairs, first in Chicago, and then in many states. A successful fair was operated in Manchester.

With these funds well-equipped hospitals were established in the South and wagon loads of necessities were driven where rail transportation was not possible. Steamboats were outfitted for hospitals on southern rivers, staffed by women.

The Catholic Sisters performed untold service in hospitals. They were the only trained persons before the war in their small private hospitals. Also, freed Negro slaves nursed Negro troops and performed other duties such as cooking and laundry in hospitals.

Only one nurse enlisted from New Hampshire, Miss Harriet Patricia Dame of Concord. She was born in Barnstead. At the age of forty-six she joined the Second New Hampshire Regiment as an army nurse. She was one of the most noted in the war. Captured at the Second Battle of Bull Run, she was soon released. She was later at the Battle of Gettysburg. In 1864 she was appointed matron of the Eighteenth Hospital Corps in Washington. After the war, from 1867 to 1895, she was a clerk in the Treasury Department in Washington. At eighty years of age she was still attending the reunions of the veterans. She camped with the regiment, always ready with a pot of coffee, beef tea, or warm clothing. She died in Concord on April 24, 1900. Her portrait now hangs in the State House.

Women served as spies on both sides, some times disguised as men, and some four hundred women were soldiers in the Northern army. Several Southern women accompanied their officer husbands upon the battlefield.

AN INCIDENT IN THE CIVIL WAR

When President Lincoln called for an army in 1861, a lad named Page disappointedly saw his friends depart for the army. His parents were ill and he was their only support.

Within the following two years the parents had died and young Page enlisted in the same regiment and joined his friends in a camp during the winter of 1863.

To keep his soldiers busy General Gates ordered them to cut the trees in a cypress swamp for a barrier to surround the camp. Immediately young Page was ordered to fell trees.

Fresh from a northern winter, the humid sunshine exhausted the untrained soldier and he sat for rest upon a stump. An officer demanded why he was not obeying orders. When he attempted to explain, he was sent to the guardhouse.

The same situation continued the next day, but Page would not chop trees. Somehow General Gates learned about disobedient Page. The kindly general sent for the lad who appeared at the general's tent with downcast eyes.

He listened to a lecture about disobedience to orders, then suddenly looked into General Gates' eyes and said, "I came down here to fight after my parents died, but I cannot cut trees in this sun. I have trees to cut at home. I am ready to fight."

Pleased by the lad's honesty, General Gates replied, "We shall find other work for you to do."

His friends recommended Page for his ability to drive horses and he was assigned to the Medicine Wagon that served first aid to wounded men on the battlefield. Without fear, Page went as ordered however the cannon balls or bullets fell.

In the winter of 1864 the regiment was again in camp in the deep south. Southern farmers were permitted to sell their produce to the soldiers. One of them saw one of the mules in Page's team and offered to buy it for twenty-five dollars.

Page said, "I cannot steal a mule from the government." The farmer continued to raise his price until it became fifty dollars. Page became indignant with the constant demand of the Southerner and finally said, "Your fifty dollars sounds good to me. I will try to get your mule for you."

"If I can get your mule, I will pin a white paper on that big tree in the gully. You will meet me there at midnight. I will put the halter into your hand and say 'Here is your mule.' You will put the fifty dollars into my hand and say 'Here is your money.' " The farmer consented to the bargain.

Several days later the white paper was pinned to the tree. The farmer arrived at midnight. According to the agreement, Page put the halter into the Southerner's hand and said, "Here is your mule," and the Southerner put the money into Page's hand and said, "Here is your money." The farmer led the mule to a cabin in the woods.

The following morning the Southerner told a Negro boy to take food and water to a mule in the cabin telling him that nothing was to be told about this mule. The Negro obeyed but was soon back to ask, "Where you git that mule? Looks like your Old Jake."

The farmer rushed to the cabin and there stood Old Jake. His anger grew hot as he appeared at the camp and demanded loudly for General Gates.

At the tent of the general he told that a soldier had stolen his mule and sold the animal back to him for fifty dollars. General Gates said, "My soldiers do not steal. Do you know the name of this soldier?"

"Yes, his name is Page." General Gates remembered Page and sent for him. When Page appeared, the General said, "This man says that you stole his mule."

Page said, "No, I did not steal his mule. I told him if I could get his mule, I would. I would pin a white paper on the big tree in the gully and he would meet me at midnight. I would put the halter into his hand and say 'Here is your mule.' He would put the money into my hand and say 'Here is your money.'

"We did as agreed. I told him it was his mule." The general told the Southerner, "I told you my soldiers do not steal. You leave my camp and never come here again. Page, you keep the money."

Years later General Gates attended a campfire in Page's home town and a fellow veteran told this tale as was customary at these gatherings.

Page remarked, "If I had supposed anybody would come home and tell this story, I would not have done it." The gray-haired general remembered Page.

THE GOOD OLD
HORSE AND BUGGY DAYS

After the Civil War New Hampshire enjoyed an era of prosperity that is often described as the "Gud ole days." Business and travel increased, education improved, and daily living was more comfortable.

The textile mills in Manchester, Dover, and Nashua wove millions of yards of cotton goods, clipper schooners slipped down the ways of the shipyards in Portsmouth and Exeter, and tons of granite were quarried in Concord.

In the larger towns, industries flourished in shoe factories, woolen and knitting mills, machine shops, and glove and hosiery establishments.

Forests were furnishing trees for lumber, paper, and wood products such as ladders, bobbins, barrels, tubs, and furniture. Every village still had its saw and gristmill and the blacksmith was a necessity.

The fertile meadows produced corn, grains, and vegetables. The pastures grazed thousands of cattle and sheep with their dairy products and wool always in demand.

This was the time when summer boarders filled the large hotels and boarding houses. This called for improved transportation by the railroads, such as express trains, parlor cars, and restaurants.

The famous Abbot and Downing coaches ran along the beautiful valleys both daily and for coaching parties. In 1869 the cog railway was erected to the summit of Mount Washington, an invention by Sylvester Marsh of Campton.

Daily living became increasingly comfortable. An adequate water supply at an elevation that permitted sewers to be installed into homes brought running water and bathrooms, although the tubs were lined with tin. Miles of tracks were laid and horsecars ran along city streets and into the suburbs.

Pumps forced water from wells into homes where there were no mountain springs to permit gravity flow through pipe lines.

Housewives welcomed improvements. The small, low cook stove was replaced by the "range" with four or six covers, a reservoir on the back that held three gallons of hot water, and a large oven that an experienced cook learned to regulate by the number of sticks of wood in the firebox.

The heavy iron kettles and pottery dishes became tin with varying thickness for boiling or baking. There were pails, dippers, and cups in many sizes.

Shopping became easy for the housekeeper. Grocers purchased their goods by the barrel: sugar, flour, cornmeal, crackers, and molasses. A grocer's clerk called in the morning at the kitchen door for orders that he delivered in the afternoon in paper bags. Packaging was not known. There was a charge account because husbands handled the pocketbook and few wives saw a dime.

In the larger localities a milkman's wagon with three-gallon cans of milk delivered the number of quarts that the housewife ordered at five cents per quart. The housewife provided the container. She usually skimmed cream from the whole milk.

In villages many families kept a cow and sold milk to neighbors who called for it at five cents per quart for whole milk and three cents for skimmed.

Refrigeration in the larger localities was made possible by the iceman who delivered a few pounds into a zinc-lined icebox as needed. In the villages, ice from ponds was stored in the winter in large cakes covered with sawdust from the mill. Many families stored their year's supply. Cellars with their soil bottoms were cool in summer and free from freezing in the winter.

Swarms of flies were everywhere. The cotton mills wove a netting that was tacked upon window frames and screen doors annually until wire screens were invented.

With the exception of the crowded cities. vegetable gardens thrived everywhere. Grape arbors and large orchards produced red Baldwins, brown Russets, and yellow Sweetings. Wild berries were free for the picking and delicious shagbark walnut, chestnut, and butternut trees grew in various areas and were usually free for the gathering. Nutting parties were fun after the fall frosts caused the nuts to fall.

Education improved with high schools opening in the larger places and the towns acquiring the former academies. From the rural villages students paid a small tuition and many rented rooms in the homes of families and "boarded themselves" from Monday to Friday.

Hospitals were established in the larger towns and new names such as appendicitis and pneumonia were heard, although the illnesses were not new. Girls trained for nursing.

Churches were active with two Sabbath services. Sunday Schools flourished. Church suppers were social gatherings with baked beans, relishes, cold meats, cakes, and pies at ten cents per person. If oyster stew or chicken pie was served, the price was twenty-five cents.

Politics were usually Republican.

Some women began to ask for the vote.

Such were the last horse and buggy days in New Hampshire a century ago.

A mail stage advertisement in 1826

{6}

Paths of Commerce

EARLY COMMERCE
BY THE BARTER SYSTEM

To exist without money today is unthinkable, yet three hundred years ago the early settlers in New Hampshire seldom saw hard money, meaning in that day mostly English or Spanish coin.

Until his sudden death in 1635, John Mason supplied all necessities to his three settlements in exchange for their fishing. After that, the heads of families acquired items for their households by exchanging or bartering their personal property.

The farmer raised corn, hay, beef, and pork while his wife wove woolen cloth. These were exchanged for imported goods with the merchants who in turn traded with English dealers.

The hunter traded his deer hides with the cobbler for shoes and the cobbler traded the hides with the tanner for leather. The farmer took his corn to the miller who ground his meal for part of the corn and the miller sold to everybody. The forester provided the sawmills with logs and the sawmills made clapboards and barrels for exchange with outside traders. Thus it was possible to exist without money.

In 1641 the four towns in New Hampshire united with the government of Massachusetts under their charter from England in which there was a permit for that colony to coin money.

After the population numbered about twenty-five thousand people, the General Court at Boston appointed Captain John Hull as mint-master to coin all of the money for the colony.

English coins were gold or silver in pounds, shillings, and

sixpence. Spanish money was silver dollars, worth four shillings and a sixpence in English money.

The wampum of the Indians, made of clamshells, was accepted in payment for goods. A belt of white wampum was valued at five shillings and one of black wampum at ten shillings.

Captain Hull was authorized to manufacture the shilling, sixpence, and threepence coins. On one side they had the date 1652 and on the other the figure of a pine tree. He received a shilling for every twenty that he coined.

People furnished their old silver, such as tankards, cans, mugs, broken spoons, buttons, buckles, and hilts of swords all tossed into the melting pot.

Captain Hull became so wealthy that he gave a dowry to his daughter of her weight in pine tree shillings. Most of the coins were made of silver bullion that the English explorers found in South America among the Spaniards and brought to Massachusetts.

During the period of union with Massachusetts, until 1679, the settlers of New Hampshire used their old silver for pine tree shillings and sixpence. In time the trade in masts and other lumber products introduced bills of credit that replaced money between the English merchants and the colony.

The French and Indian Wars brought a heavy debt to the treasury of New Hampshire and for temporary relief, bills of credit were issued by the legislature. These soon depreciated but were redeemed when England paid some of her war claims owed to the colony.

Then came the American Revolution and New Hampshire issued large amounts of paper which became almost worthless. In 1781 the value of one hundred paper dollars was but one silver dollar.

Also the Continental Congress began to issue paper money which depreciated. "Not worth a Continental" is an expression even now familiar.

Finally in 1794 a law was passed in New Hampshire that

all money should be in dollars and cents in the state of New Hampshire. This was five years after George Washington became president of the United States.

The first bank in New Hampshire was established in Portsmouth in 1792, called the New Hampshire Bank, with a capital of $160,000.

The first savings bank in New Hampshire was incorporated at Portsmouth in 1823 and the first national bank in the United States applied to Portsmouth for its charter under the act of 1863.

In 1863, New Hampshire had fifty-two banks. In 1874 there were forty-three national banks in the state and sixty-eight savings banks with 963,938 depositors holding $30,214,585.

Since then the value of the dollar has changed vastly. At that time if a man had $10,000 in a savings bank, he was considered "well-to-do."

Banking customs have made great changes also. Unless a woman possessed an account in her own name in a bank, her signature was not honored upon a bank check.

Few women handled a dollar—men carried the pocketbooks. On the farms in New Hampshire the farmer's wife usually cared for the hens and sometimes considered that the "egg money" belonged to her to exchange at the store for goods that she wished to purchase.

Even forty years ago in New Hampshire the bank account of a family was in the name of the husband and the signature of his wife was not honored. The joint account is somewhat recent—if the signature of the wife is registered at the bank, the names of both husband and wife are printed upon the bank's checks.

INDIAN TRAILS
BECOME THE EARLY ROADS

The future is the past. The truth of this remark is proved

by the story of the early roads of New Hampshire.

A highway engineer should remember when he is driving on the Daniel Webster Highway that he is on one of the oldest pathways in this country.

About two thousand years ago the Abanaki Indians traced this path along the bank of the Merrimack River because fish and game were plentiful. Historians believe that these people came from Canada through Maine, then inland up the valleys of the Saco and Cocheco rivers.

Wearing their moccasins of hides, said to have been the best footwear to be designed, on snowshoes, or in their lightweight canoes, the Indians made the Penacook Trail, Route 3; the Ossipee Trail, Route 25; the Sunapee Trail, Route 103, and the Connecticut River Trail, Route 10.

Route 25 twists from Cornish, Maine, to Bradford, Vermont. Also, a water route was followed from the Piscataqua River across the Cocheco River to Lake Winnipesauke, along a short path to the Squam Lakes, to the Pemigewasset and Baker rivers, by a chain of lakes to the Connecticut River and across Vermont by different routes to Canada with short carries, so-called, between the lakes and rivers.

The English arrived in 1623. By 1675 the Indians decided that white men were not welcome. After another fifty years of warfare, the Indians were dead or had fled to Canada leaving their language in the names of trails, mountains, and lakes.

The Post Road from Portsmouth to Boston was built in 1696. The king appointed William Neal to be the first postmaster general in America in 1693. Postmaster Neal came to Boston to plan for mail to pass between Virginia and Boston weekly. He appealed to the Provincial Council of New Hampshire "for an extension of the service to Piscataqua." The Council approved leaving the details to the postmaster general, but believed that "every person should pay for his own letter."

The roads were rough and in winter the rider sometimes changed from horseback to snowshoes. After 1720 young farmers began to move inland. So-called axmen cut a road between Kingston and Chester that was later extended to Loudon and Canterbury.

Meanwhile, from Fort Dummer on the border in Massachusetts, settlers were moving up the Connecticut Valley. In 1736 the towns of Concord, Canterbury, and Charlestown were building log cabins and small forts to protect their settlers from the French and Indians who came from Canada.

In 1744 Governor Benning Wentworth authorized a "scouting path" be cut between Fort Number Four and Fort Contoocut in Salisbury which was along the old Sunapee Trail of the Penacook Indians.

In 1759 this rough path was widened for a military road to permit cannon to be brought from Boston to Charlestown.

By the close of the French and Indian Wars communication across the colony was possible. The roads were narrow cart paths, possible for oxen. Men rode horseback, often with a wife and one or two small children sitting on a small cushion on the saddle behind the husband. Hanging on either side of the saddle were leather bags that contained food and necessary clothing.

Horse and buggy days were still twenty-five years in the future. Only in the summer months were these early roads passable. In the spring and fall, mud was deep, and in winter snowdrifts blocked the way.

I remember the story a ninety-year-old grandmother told me about her journey from Connecticut to Vermont when she was a small girl. She said she was tucked safely among the pieces of furniture cushioned by a featherbed. Her brothers walked behind the horse-drawn wagon, each leading a cow.

While we ride in comfort along the super highways, I doubt if a mental picture of those early roads is possible.

TAVERNS AND TURNPIKES

With the United States established, President Washington

ordered the first census to be taken in 1790. The population of New Hampshire was increasing and its narrow bridle paths and two-wheeled cart tracks were a hindrance to the economy.

Ancient trails of the Indians are now Routes 10, 3, and 25 and the five Province Roads: Canterbury to Charlestown, Durham to Haverhill, Portsmouth to Wolfeboro, "Dartmouth" on to Hanover, and a part of Route 16 opened the interior of the colony. County and range roads served the towns. All were narrow, muddy in the spring and fall, dusty in summer, and blocked by snow in winter.

In 1790 came an improved road surface called a turnpike. Men with money to invest formed corporations that were licensed to rebuild roads and charge a toll for passing over them. Strong gates blocked these roads about every ten miles. The gates turned usually with leather hinges upon a post set deeply into the ground and pointed at the top, called a pike. Thus the name turnpikes.

The price of the toll varied; persons walking or riding horseback, loaded wagons, cattle, sheep, and chaise were assessed a separate toll.

Travel increased rapidly, demanding accommodations for overnight and for food. Taverns soon appeared near the tollgates, two-story houses with long ells and sheds, stables, and fenced yards.

A front doorway opened into a central hall. On one side was a long tap or barroom, with a large fireplace to take long logs to hold a steady fire which was used by the teamsters and drovers. Behind this room was a dining room with long tavern tables. The kitchen was in the rear.

On the opposite side of the hall was a parlor and a smaller dining room that would be used by travelers on horses or chaise. In the rear was another dining room that was equipped with even better facilities.

Above were chambers with several beds for the hurried teamsters and single rooms for other guests. Usually these smaller rooms were not heated but warming pans and pitchers of hot water were provided by maids. Straw-filled ticks and deep featherbeds with linen sheets and wool blankets made sleeping comfortable.

Drovers often slept in the tap room before the fireplace because they were sometimes obliged to run out at any hour to quiet a herd.

The food was hearty and plentiful, served family style, and everyone helped himself to all he desired. Boiled dinners, meat and vegetable stews, chowders, corn bread, brown bread and beans, steamed puddings and pies were the common menu. Cooks became famous for their specialities.

Refrigeration was then unknown. Herds of cattle and sheep in varied numbers were driven to market in the spring and fall. Many days were required to be sure that the animals arrived in safe condition. Rest overnight demanded fenced fields and food and shelter.

Wagon loads of corn and hay followed the herds and water had to be in ready supply. On the outskirts of cities, shelters were maintained.

Flocks of turkeys were driven for the Christmas trade. These were kept together by young leaders carrying bags of corn that was scattered ahead of the flocks, in sufficient quantity, to keep them following these leaders. At sundown the birds would fly to the limbs of trees near the tavern which were usually of sufficient height so that foxes could not attack the birds. Guards were necessary throughout the night.

A new vehicle called a chaise came into use. It was a two-wheeled, one-horse carriage used for trips to town, by doctors and businessmen. This was later superseded by the buggy and two-seated carriages, called carryalls, or democrats, one and two-seaters.

Men and women began to ride to town for shopping causing stores to be opened. Gradually the so-called country store developed, which stocked every article of food, cloth, utensil, drugs, and furniture. Even webs of silk and ribbons, shoes, and bonnets were displayed, many of these imported from Europe. Green or black tea was brought from Asia and coffee beans to be ground when needed for brewing were commonly purchased.

News about the scenery spread southward as the turnpikes made traveling possible as far to the north as Haverhill and Hanover. Taverns in these towns were known far and wide. Several remain in operation today.

THE ENGINEERING SKILL IN COVERED BRIDGES

When the fishermen settled in New Hampshire, every man owned his own boat. A settler was authorized to run a ferryboat across the rivers. Until the settlers began to move inland with their ox teams, about 1725, bridges were not necessary.

Nobody remembers the name of the man who planned the first "crib" in the middle of a wide stream. When the water was low in midsummer, a wall of logs like a log cabin was anchored in midstream by filling it with rocks. More logs and rocks were added until the crib was higher than the spring flood and stone walls of either bank were built of equal height to the crib.

Four timbers stretching from the corners of the stone walls to the four corners of the crib were the foundation for the plank floor of the bridge. Heavy logs laid along the edges of the floor held the planks solidly in place, and the rustic bridge was completed.

Horse and buggy days and the turnpikes about 1790 demanded safer bridges and the covered bridge era began. Experienced craftsmen-carpenters were then living. To these men in the shipyards, and the framers of colonial homesteads and large meetinghouses, belongs the honor of the covered bridges.

These carpenters learned by experience that walls must resist stress. They also knew that a triangle of timbers firmly fastened at their joints would support greater weight than upright posts and the strongest support was a broad arch. With this knowledge covered bridges were designed.

The frame of a covered bridge consisted of two high walls that extended across a stream and cross timbers at the top for a ceiling and at the base for a foundation for the floor of the bridge. The top and bottom of the frames of the two walls were heavy timbers, called chords. Trusses connected the chords. Repeated groups of two and sometimes three long timbers were laid diagonally like a narrow letter X and were firmly mortised into the chords. Where these met and crossed at their centers, they were pinned together with oak trunnels (tree-nails) that were driven through them with mallets.

The walls were covered with boards on the outsides and a roof above protected the complicated structure from the weather. Usually openings were left in one of the sides to admit light.

Timothy Palmer, an experienced carpenter of Newburyport, Massachusetts, constructed the first covered bridge over the Merrimack River between Newbury and Amesbury in 1792 and another over the Piscataqua River in 1794. He became famous when he built a long covered bridge over the Schuylkill River at Philadelphia in 1806, another over the Susquehanna River, and a third over the Potomac River. This one stood through the Civil War.

The late George G. Clark, well-informed historian of Plymouth, told me that an aged citizen of Holderness informed him that Timothy Palmer was employed to erect the covered bridge over the Pemigewasset River between Plymouth and Holderness which washed down the river in the flood of 1813 and another over the Baker River at the site of the present Smith Bridge, about 1800.

Five covered bridges were erected later, all with the same design of triple timbered trusses: two over the Baker River, now gone, the Lafayette Bridge of 1825, now demolished, the Blair Bridge in Campton in 1828, and the present Smith Bridge in 1849 which is a copy of the first bridge of 1800.

In 1968 the Smithsonian Institution published a book containing a picture of the Timothy Palmer bridge at Washington guarded by a Civil War soldier. Its trusses are the same design as the trusses in the present Blair and Smith bridges. Both of them have been reinforced with laminated arches.

In 1820, a native New England carpenter, Theodore Burr, designed a truss combined with laminated arches which the first railroad, the Baltimore and Ohio, accepted for its covered bridges. The bridge at Bath has Burr trusses.

About 1810 Ithiel Towne, a carpenter from New Haven, Connecticut, began to build his lattice truss which he patented in 1820 and for which he charged a dollar per foot. Here two layers of plank were set diagonally opposite and about two feet apart between the chords.

The Cornish-Windsor Bridge is of lattice construction, now the property of the state. In 1866 it began as a toll bridge and the prices for crossing are still displayed at either end. Many of the remaining bridges are lattice truss design.

In 1840 William Howe introduced a truss, similar to the Timothy Palmer design, but it was strengthened with wrought iron rods extending from chord to chord with threads and nuts at each end which were supposed to be frequently tightened. The Lancaster Bridge over the Connecticut River has Howe trusses.

The approximately sixty covered bridges remaining in New Hampshire are architectural antiques. No two are alike, although those which were built by such skilled carpenters as James Tasker and James Berry display similar features.

STAGE COACHES
AND ED COX'S FINE CHESTNUTS

Coaches were introduced into the colonies long before the Revolution. Wealthy families owned them with slaves for coachmen and stableboys. After the turnpikes brought better roads, a stage line was established by a group of businessmen, running from Concord to Haverhill one day and returning the next. Later a line ran a circle from Concord to Hanover, on to Haverhill, and back down to Concord twice a week.

The equipment was two and three-seated covered wagons, and about every twenty miles stables kept relays of horses for the eighty mile route, and the longer circle, approximately three hundred miles.

The Tally-ho coach that provided seats both inside and on the top was popular for coaching trips, especially after taverns became famous for their accommodations.

In 1827 the Abbot-Downing Company began to produce the Concord Coach that used the leather thoroughbraces that gave this vehicle the reputation of "the only perfect vehicle for travel ever made."

In the entrance hall at the State Historical Library in Concord one of these ornate coaches is on display. A father and son named Borgum painted the landscapes upon the doors.

Even after the railroads, a stage line rattled through Franconia Notch in 1912 to transport guests to the Profile Hotel from the station at North Woodstock. Apparently this old coach gave great satisfaction. Town histories preserve stories of a score of famous drivers and their well-trained spans of horses.

The most well known holder of the reins was Edward Cox, a descendant of the Cox family of Holderness. His trip with General Grant and a party of ten friends between Bethlehem and the Profile Hotel is worthy of preservation in the history of stage coach days.

The Sinclair Hotel in Bethlehem was erected in 1865. It has entertained hundreds of well-known guests, one of whom was General Grant in 1869.

This tale of the famous trip is related here from the personal observation of Mr. Eugene Bowles of Franconia who, as a boy, stood on the corner at Littleton as the team made the turn toward Franconia.

When it became known in the stables that General Grant

desired to drive with his party of friends to the Profile Hotel, and that old Ed Cox was to be the driver of the Tally-ho coach, a wager was made that he could not make the fifteen-mile trip in less than two hours.

Ed Cox accepted the wager with a smile. He owned six chestnut horses with a famous lead span. He made careful preparations. First he carefully fed his horses. Then he examined every inch of his harnesses for weak spots. He fastened every bolt and nut of the "Profile Chariot."

About seven o'clock on an August evening the coach drew up before the door of the Sinclair Hotel. When General Grant saw the six horses, he pushed his cap down over his eyes and requested that he might ride outside beside Ed Cox. General Grant climbed over the wheel and braced his feet against the dashboard.

Ed Cox adjusted the reins between his fingers, with the reins to the lead span carefully fixed, and cracked his whip like a pistol shot.

Down the six-mile Bethlehem Hill dashed the vehicle with the sensitive horses obeying the driver's control. A crowd was watching at the turn in Littleton. The coach raced down the back road to Franconia, through the woods, and up the three-mile hill without changing speed, past Echo Lake, and around the circle to the doorway of the Profile House. The time that was registered by telegram was exactly fifty-eight minutes. Ed Cox won the wager.

General Grant enjoyed every minute of the trip, but he was concerned about the tired horses. Ed Cox knew his steeds and they suffered no harm from the run.

When General Grant knew that the team was not injured, he ordered a whip with silver bands around the stock, engraved with the driver's name and that of his own. Its lash was twelve feet in length and all of this was enclosed in a case of leather.

This gift was kept in the Historical Library on display for many years. A member of the Cox family is supposed to possess it now.

CANALS AND RAILROADS

Transportation in New Hampshire was managed by sail-boats along the coast and by horses and oxen on the highways until the beginning of the nineteenth century. The products of the northern farms were carried in wagons drawn by spans of horses over the Coos Province Road to Portsmouth.

In 1807 the Middlesex Canal was completed around the Amoskeag Falls at Manchester, and about the same time canals around the falls at Bellows Falls and White River Junction opened the Connecticut River to its mouth.

Flat bottomed boats and rafts floated loads of produce to the seacoast where the boats were usually sold. The rafts, loaded with supplies, were poled upstream by husky men.

Usually two men thrust long poles into the bed of the stream and pushed from the rear while two men at the front both pushed and guided the raft. The speed attained was about that of a loaded wagon—and for less money.

The canals were used until railroads were constructed in New Hampshire in 1838. As early as 1630 wooden rails were laid upon the surface of roads to help the movement of heavy loads. They were called tramroads. After 150 years somebody thought to cover the wooden rails with iron and flange to prevent the wheels from running off the rails. Later the flange was attached to the wheels.

James Watts, who discovered the power of steam, began to suggest that a steam carriage might be invented, and a man in Philadelphia actually patented a steam wagon. In 1784 Watts patented a locomotive.

Improvements followed until 1822 when Robert Stevenson substituted steam for horsepower.

The first railroad in New Hampshire connected Lowell, Massachusetts, with Nashua in 1838 and extended to Concord in 1842, on to Plymouth in 1850, and towards Woodsville the following year.

Steam was generated in the small engines with wood

piled high on the tender at every station. Black smoke poured from the mushroom-shaped smokestack with its top covered by a fine netted screen to catch some of the sparks which often set fires along the track. Turntables were built at terminals for both engines and cars (until the backs of the seats in the passenger coaches were made reversible).

Restaurants were maintained at stations where trains stopped noon and evening. A famous place was at the Pemigewasset Hotel in Plymouth. Here the express trains between Montreal and Boston met at noon and five P.M. Scores of the famous individual chicken pies were demanded daily.

In the summer months tourists left the trains for lunch and the platform would be filled with citizens of the town to see the styles the summer travelers wore. Stages for Franconia Notch met these trains.

Passenger cars were not the comfortably arranged equipment of modern time. The soot from the wood-burning engine poured back over the cars. To open a window meant a smoke and cinder filled compartment, for screens were not provided in the early years. A small stove stood near the door for heat in the winter, the backs of the seats were too low for heads to rest upon, and ice water was not supplied. Brakemen turned brakes at every stop, and jerks and bumps were expected by passengers.

Corporations made up of private investors provided the funds for the railroads as a rule. Valuable meadows along the rivers where the tracks were built were taken from the farms, regardless of objections.

In the Connecticut Valley sheep raising was becoming a lucrative business. Farmers objected to the railroad because they claimed the smoke from the wood-burning engines would soil the wool of the sheep. Teamsters had great difficulty controlling their horses when a train passed and cattle ran in wild fright in the pastures. Many men purchased railroad stocks and lost every cent while others earned dividends.

Objections soon disappeared when, among other things,

the advantage of daily mail service became apparent. The farmer found that he could arrange with the paper boy on the train to toss off the Boston morning newspaper to a youngster who waited to catch it as he stood by the pasture fence. The contrast of living before and after railroads is difficult to imagine today.

THE EARLY DAYS
OF THE TEXTILE INDUSTRY

Cascading brooks and waterfalls are beautiful and also forceful. This inexpensive power turned the waterwheels for the sawmills and gristmills in the early days of New Hampshire.

The nimble fingers of the women carded the wool, turned the spinning wheels, and threaded the looms for the household textiles until 1800.

Although Archibald Stark and his son John used the Amoskeag Falls in the Merrimack River, the first person who fully realized this power was Samuel Blodgett.

To harness this source of energy he began the upper canal from the river in 1794 and completed the work in 1807 at an expense of $125,000.

When he visited the cotton mills in Manchester, England, he prophesied that Derryfield would become the Manchester of the new world. In recognition of his foresight, the city was later named Manchester.

A cotton mill was opened in 1805 and the Amoskeag in 1810, which became the largest cotton mill in the world. The Merrimack River turned the greatest number of spindles in the world.

Nashua had its Indian Head Mill, Dover its Pacific, and Somersworth its Great Works, with about fifty smaller works in many towns by 1850.

Unbleached sheeting over a yard in width was purchased by housewives to be bleached by several methods and sewed with two lengths for a sheet because the price was less than for bleached material. Years later wide sheeting was woven.

Prints were produced about twenty-seven inches in width. Amoskeag specialized in ginghams, in stripes and squares, and later the thinner Scotch ginghams became most popular. A few yards of these materials would be difficult to find today.

About 1830 immigrants from Ireland by the thousands became the weavers in the mills of New England. The Scotch-Irish in the city did not welcome these Catholic immigrants. They remembered the persecutions of their ancestors in Ireland.

A small Catholic chapel was erected and the Scotch-Irish objected with mob violence. The supporting timbers of the floor were sawed almost apart so that the floor settled when the audience was present, although no injuries were reported.

Finally an influential citizen decided that this trouble should end. He stood with his gun at the door of the chapel and threatened to shoot if anyone of the objecting crowd advanced toward the door.

Realizing that this threat would be certain, the mob dispersed and decided to cease its opposition. At that time Manchester was not an incorporated city and apparently was without an active police force.

The first mills that might be called textiles were fulling mills for the purpose of smoothing the surface of homespun cloth and shrinking it by dampening and pressing so that the cloth would hold its shape when made into garments.

Machines for carding wool, spinning it into yarn, and power looms were rapidly introduced about 1825. One of the first was established in Campton on the Mad River in 1826. At first it was for carding only, then a spinning mill for knitting yarns, and finally it wove heavy goods that were used for workmen's pants which gained a reputation for never wearing out. Its final product was beautiful yarns for sweaters—before it closed in 1964. In 1850 sixty woolen mills were operating, many in the northern towns. Today woolen mills are producing beautiful suitings in modern weaves.

This textile industry brought a demand for wool so that farmers, especially in the Connecticut Valley, began to keep thousands of sheep. A merino breed and later other kinds of wool were in demand. At one period over 600,000 sheep were found in the state.

After western ranches were offered to young farmers from the east, sheep were herded there and this industry rapidly disappeared from New Hampshire.

Long lines of sheep were once driven to the Boston markets. A tradition existed that thousands starved when the farmers were unable to sell their wool because Australian wool knocked the price from under domestic production.

The woolen mills wove a loose, soft flannel. Babies wore long petticoats of white, lightweight flannel and outside jackets because homes were not warmly heated. No person of eighty or more years will forget that bright red that mothers sewed for undershirts and long pants causing "red flannel itch" every fall when it was first donned. Every small girl proudly wore a bright red or a light blue flannel dress for best.

A hundred years have slipped away. The cotton mills have gone south where the cotton grows, textiles are synthetics and may even contain glass, wood, or fibers of a strange plant.

The cascades and waterfalls still flow in beauty down the valleys.

OUR WATER
IS HEALTH, BEAUTY, INDUSTRY

This book has told the story about the settlement and development of New Hampshire but the prehistoric narrative remains untold. Through uncounted centuries, Mother Nature has prepared the land for human habitation.

Perhaps the greatest natural resource is water that is abundantly supplied because of the geographical location along the coast of the Atlantic Ocean.

Water exists in gas, liquid, and solid conditions. When the sun shines directly upon the sea it lifts water by evaporation into the atmosphere where it condenses into fog or clouds late in the afternoon.

Wafted inland by the east wind, the clouds hang above the cool summits of the mountains where they condense into rain. Down the slopes the rain flows with a small amount stopping at Lake of the Clouds near the summit of Mount Washington or Lonesome Lake on Cannon Mountain.

Much of the rain sinks into the soil down to bedrock. The remainder runs into rills, to brooks and rivers, and back to the ocean to complete the cycle.

Along the valleys of the bedrock the underground water runs seeking its level until it bubbles up through the soil to fill the Squam Lakes, Winnipesaukee, and springs that rise even to the summits of the foothills.

Southward toward the coastal plain the underground water spreads into streams that fill wells, both natural and driven, that may be tapped in almost every location for a pure supply of water for domestic use.

The surface rainwater drains into valleys, brooks, and converges into rivers such as the Connecticut, Merrimack, Saco, and Piscataqua.

The first settlers at Portsmouth in 1631 began to use the power of their small waterfalls to turn the waterwheels for their grist and sawmills. Transportation was by sailboats on the rivers and along the seacoast. Water was a necessity for survival.

At the beginning of the nineteenth century power-looms were invented and woolen and cotton mills were operated by the power of the waterfalls in the rivers, bringing the prosperity of industry to New Hampshire.

Steam was applied to machines, and railroads made their network throughout the state. Then came electricity and waterfalls generated this new power. The population rapidly increased demanding water systems for domestic use. Thoughtless man filled the rivers with waste from sewers and pollution became an ugly word.

Winter with its zero cold, snowstorms, and ice created problems. Suddenly a new million dollar industry made a marvelous change in the twentieth century. Skiing demanded roads to be cleared for travel as in summer. Winter resorts opened where hills were snowcovered.

Suddenly winter departs. Spring awakens in April and May to release the stored-up water of ice and snow. Ice melts and breaks up in the streams, snow melts into brooks, and then streams become bank full—overflowing into meadows, bringing renewed richness to fertile fields.

The landscape changes with the twigs of the hardwoods covered with tiny blossoms, Pussywillows and the alders are draped with clusters of tasseled blossoms. Arbutus open their pink and white clusters of fragrance, many varieties of mayflowers open beneath the evergreens.

Then the vivid greens of the tiny leaves on the trees burst their brown buds and the landscape becomes a fairy land of delicate colors. Autumn colors are brilliant but the landscape in May has unsurpassed fascination for those who have endured a long winter.

This is the month to see the waterfalls of the brooks along the highways that the tourists in summer miss. In May sheets of white foam cascade down the cliffs and ripple along the roadsides.

At the southern entrance to Pinkham Notch are the Jackson Cascades. Northward, signs point to Glen Ellis Falls where the descent of the stairs is rewarded by the sight of sixty-four feet of falling white water.

Drive on to the Pinkham Notch Hut and walk up an easy pathway to the Crystal Cascade to see another fall of white bubbles that fans widely from top to base. Thompson Falls and two others splash down the Carter Range and are worth the short walks to find them.

At the head of Crawford Notch are two cascades that fall down the side of Mount Jackson in sight of the highway and further south, short walks reveal the famous Diana's Bath and the Arethusa Falls.

The Flume falls in Franconia Notch and the circular pathway requires time to enjoy, whether taken from either end or in both directions. The Basin in spring is spectacular. Cross the bridge at the Basin and wander into the forest where two brooks fall in cascades into the Basin. Streams that are dry in summer are waterfalls off the Franconia Range in May.

To New Hampshire, water is health, beauty, and industry combined.

THE GRANITE STATE'S MINERAL RESOURCES

Minerals are defined as the chemical elements of our world, although today we think of the word in relation to elements that are found in mines. New Hampshire contains over two hundred minerals, more than any other state.

The first ore to be mined was bog iron, discovered in Newmarket about 1710. Archibald MacPhaedris of Portsmouth offered the Scotch miners twelve acres of land if they would migrate to Portsmouth. More bog iron was found in Gilmanton and Tamworth before the American Revolution.

A tradition remains in Tamworth that links of the 700-foot chain that was placed across the Hudson River below West Point in 1779 to prevent the British from ascending the river were made in Tamworth. The links were transported by oxen to Rutland and the Champlain Valley. Fragments are now in museums at Albany and West Point.

There are iron mines at Franconia, and ore containing gold, silver, and copper was mined on Cannon Mountain. An abandoned gold mine is at Benton.

Recently an experienced prospector is reported to have

panned the gravel in several brooks in the vicinity of Colebrook and occasionally discovered nuggets of gold that he
sold for twenty-five dollars.

Graphite was mined in Bristol in sufficient amounts to sell
to manufacturers of lead pencils. Along the eastern shore of
Newfound Lake the rocks contain hundreds of garnets the
size of pin heads—with now and then a ruby red gem for a
jeweler's use.

In Acworth beryl crystals are found that resemble emer-
alds and topaz of semi-precious value, and others of green-
ish or bluish colors that are collectors' items.

New Hampshire is truly the Granite State, famous for its
quarries at Concord that have supplied the walls of many
buildings far and wide. Its glassy quartz, dull gray or white
feldspar, and shining mica are a conglomerate or found in
separate forms.

A clear white quartz crystal, eight inches in length and
one in diameter, is valued at $5,000 and specimens of deli-
cate blue or pink crystals are semiprecious gems to the jew-
elers.

Small granite rocks of three to ten inches in diameter
named geodes are hollow and lined with quartz crystals of
several colors; amethyst of special beauty, but pink and
white exist.

Feldspar in chunks of dull white is mined to use in the
manufacture of choice table dishes and deep pink specimens are collectors' items.

Mica mines in Groton and Warren produce clear sheets
that cleave into paper thin layers that were used for windows in oven doors and in openings in the sides of coal
stoves to reveal the glowing fire.

Mica is an insulating agent in electrical apparatus and
scrap mica is used in roofing material. In recent years mica
mines have produced annual incomes of $3,800,000 although
they are closed at present.

The most famous mine today is located at Grafton—the
Ruggles Mine that is said to contain the largest variety of

minerals in this country. It produced tons of white feldspar, copper, beryl, and uranium. It is said to be the oldest mica mine in America.

The discovery of almost pure uranium was made by a geologist of Laconia, Mayer J. Kassner, and Walter Shortel, the chemist at Scott and Williams factory in Laconia, about 1935.

The two scientists searched the Ruggles Mine for radioactive elements and discovered the ore named autumite with their ultra violet ray from a lamp which Mr. Kassner designed.

After geiger counters were invented, with scientists of Dartmouth and Harvard, they searched the White Mountains for radioactive elements with success.

In 1964 a team of scientists from Rice University in Houston, Texas, discovered a nuclear fuel called thorium in the granite of the White Mountains which increases the amount of nuclear fuel by millions of tons.

This fuel is not needed now and would be too expensive today. New Hampshire is a storehouse for the future.

Many college students are becoming rock hounds during their summer vacations and are finding specimens of value occasionally. They visit many of the old mines that are scattered about the state.

Times change. Sand and gravel once supposed to be useless are today a business of thousands of dollars annually. Minerals are worthy of observation for young and old in New Hampshire.

Maxfield Parrish designed this poster for the state in 1936.

{7}

Minds and Hands

THE POTTERS OF EARLY DAYS

In these days of modern kitchen appliances, we seldom think of earlier days in New Hampshire when even the most elemental utensils needed for cooking were hard to come by.

For example, women were faced every day with the need to cook in the old brick oven beside the fireplace. Metal pots and pans were rare. Pottery made from the earth of the Granite State provided the answer.

The first potter in New England was a Quaker named William A. Osbourne in Salem, Massachusetts, in 1635. He was an expert craftsman who taught his four sons to follow in his trade.

In 1639 Salem granted ten acres of land to four Quakers for the purpose of producing pottery and glass. William Southwick and Joseph Osbourne made pottery there for many years and their descendants continued for a century.

In 1775 in the town of Danvers, once a part of Salem, seventy-five potters were working and seventeen of them were Osbournes.

To become an expert potter required seven years of training. Pottery is porous and a glaze is necessary to render it leak-proof. We are told that the early redware, as it was called, was glazed with salt. After the pots were heated very hot in the kiln, the door was opened and salt was tossed into the interior of the pots. Then they continued to bake until the chemicals in the salt were spread over the surface of the inside of the pots. Thus a brown glaze was formed to prevent leaks.

The first utensils were called pots, about a foot in height, with a broad base, and circular walls one-half inch in thickness and six inches in diameter.

Flaring shapes were made for baking brown bread and puddings. There were bean pots with covers, milk pans that contained two gallons, pitchers, and finally jugs of many sizes.

Although their names are forgotten, there were potters in Portsmouth and Dover in those early days. In 1785 Jacob Osbourne removed to Loudon, New Hampshire, where he erected a large home and a pottery on Osbourne Hill. Several of his sons built their homes in the vicinity and followed the craft for many years.

A grandson, Elijah Osbourne, opened a pottery in Gonic (Rochester), where he developed a greenish-yellow glaze that he used to produce a mottled effect. By scattering spots of the yellow over a brown glaze and then baking the piece again, the yellow mixed with the brown to make the mottled effect. Elijah's kiln would fire 300 pieces at one baking.

Potters were in Exeter in 1742 and a family named Dodge was there in 1770. The claim was made that the clay used in Exeter was the finest grade in the state.

Peter Clark came from Massachusetts to Lyndeboro, New Hampshire, at the time of the Revolution with his four sons who followed their father's craft and became potters in several towns. Daniel Clark opened his pottery in Millville (Concord) about 1791.

Peter Flanders trained his seven years in the Clark Pottery. He was born in Concord and when a young man drove a stage between Concord and Haverhill. He is said to have made in Millville a large plate with a reddish glaze that is regarded as one of the important specimens in the pottery collection of the New Hampshire Historical Society. He inscribed a date on his plate, never a custom among New Hampshire potters. This reads "Concord September 12, 1807."

In 1816 Peter Flanders opened a tavern at the head of the

Mayhew Turnpike in Plymouth and erected a pottery a few rods to the north beside the Haverhill Turnpike. Evidently he was successful, because he had a sales room near his pottery.

In a collection of pottery at the public library in Plymouth is a rum ring made by Peter Flanders. Its glaze is a mottled yellow and brown. A two-handled vase by Flanders in this collection has a gray glaze of unusual beauty.

Boscawen became a pottery center with famous potters named Jeremiah Burpee, Alexander Gill, and several Osbournes.

Mehitable Osbourne married Isaac Lowell at Loudon and they established a pottery in the forest in Orange where they continued in business as late as 1885.

About 1850, tinware was available for baking and pottery was no longer in demand. Several potters finally made plant pots in attractive designs. Many will remember the shallow, fluted-top pots that grandmother hung in her window in the winter containing ivy or the pink oxalis with its clover-like leaves.

Collectors today find cream jugs and pitchers in many designs with a glossy brown glaze both inside and out.

Jugs were used in the late nineteenth century in most families. Does anyone possess one of the quart-size brown jugs that tapered toward the bottom and originated the old song, "Little Brown Jug, I Love Thee?" This would be a collectors' item of high value.

OUR REVERE BELLS STILL RING OUT

We are told that the bell, inscribed "Proclaiming Liberty throughout the land" that hung in the tower of Independence Hall in Philadelphia, rang on July 4, 1776, to announce the Delcaration of Independence. Since that date, bells have celebrated independence on the Fourth of July and the bell at Philadelphia is "The Liberty Bell."

In New Hampshire there are Revere Bells. The Revere

Copper and Brass Company has preserved a stock book that lists 3,398 bells by number that were cast by the Revere foundry.

The only bell cast by Paul Revere which hangs in New Hampshire is in the tower of the town hall at Milford. This is inscribed "Revere, 1802." Its number is 50 on the list. This bell has tolled at the time of the death of every president of the United States with the exception of George Washington.

Joseph Revere became a partner with his father, and nine bells from this partnership are in New Hampshire bearing the inscription Revere & Son and the date.

The Revere & Son bell dated 1811 and number 123 was brought by ox team from the dooryard at the home of Paul Revere and hung between two trees until the steeple on the Hopkinton Congregational Church was completed. A crack developed on either side of this bell. These were welded and the bell still rings from the tower in which it was hung 160 years ago.

In the tower at the town hall in North Hampton hangs number 156, dated 1815, as it was originally cast. At Lord's Hill in Effingham hangs number 233, purchased in 1821.

In the beautiful steeple at Hancock is number 236 with its wooden yoke strongly bound with well-bolted iron bands. Two others are at Newport. Number 265 was purchased by the Baptist Church on July 28, 1852, and, in less than three weeks, number 275 by the Congregational Church.

At New London the small Revere & Son bell, dated 1826 and numbered 339 indicates that business was active in the Revere Foundry on Lynn Street in Boston.

Paul Revere III was a member of the firm with his father until 1800 when he established his own foundry with his trademark, Revere, Boston. Four bells with his inscription are in New Hampshire. The first is at Hampstead, dated 1809.

At Chatham is a Revere, Boston, bell without date and no record exists about when it was purchased. Another at Wolfeboro was first hung in the tower of Brewster Academy which was erected in 1820 and no records are preserved about the time of its purchase. It is now in the tower of the town hall to sound the hours for the town clock.

Two Revere, Boston, bells are in Keene. One is supposed to have been recast in 1829. The second bell is listed in the stock book as number 387. This bell was purchased in 1828 by the Baptist Church. Since Paul Revere III died in 1813, probably Joseph Revere made the bell before 1828.

Recast Revere bells are at Exeter, Charlestown, Franklin, Lempster, East Jaffrey, Greenfield, Deerfield, and Antrim. The bell at Newington was a gift from Newington, England, in 1712. After it cracked it was recast by Paul Revere & Son in 1804.

Paul Revere became a bell-ringer at the age of thirteen when a chime of eight bells was installed in the steeple of the Old North Church on Salem Street in 1744. His father was a goldsmith.

Paul learned to be an engraver and also a metalsmith for gold, silver, and copper. He established a foundry on Lynn Street in Boston.

When the bell at the Brick Church that Paul Revere attended cracked, he recast it but its tone was sharp. He continued to cast over one hundred bells before he sent his son Joseph abroad to learn to cast perfect bells.

Until 1801 the firm was Revere & Son, then Paul Revere removed to Canton, Massachusetts, and purchased a mill where he rolled copper for the navy. He died in 1818. Joseph continued the foundry in Boston until 1826, then removed to Canton where he died in 1868.

Many apprentices learned the trade of casting bells at the foundry in Boston, among them George H. Holbrook, Henry N. Hooper, and Warren Blake.

Holbrook established a foundry in Medford, Massachusetts, and cast thousands of bells, many for missions in California. Blake joined Joseph Revere in 1820 and continued until Joseph removed to Canton.

A new company, called the Boston Copper Company,

formed and three of its bells are in Acworth, Portsmouth, and Jaffrey. This firm manufactured the first chime bells in 1825.

The Revere Copper and Brass Company is still in operation.

THE JOYS OF MUSIC

There were few posibilities for amusement among the first settlers in New Hampshire. If they were in the mood, singing was a pastime.

The oldest folk song now remembered is, "O Dear, What Can the Matter Be?" said to have been composed by King Henry VIII to tease a young girl at his court.

At their Sabbath services, the settlers sang psalms. The minister or a leader sang a line and the audience repeated it and so they sang line by line for the entire song.

As new immigrants arrived they introduced new music. The well-known nursery rhymes, such as "Hey Diddle" were remembered by Mrs. Elizabeth Goose of Boston and her son-in-law printed them in 1719 as "Mother Goose's Melodies."

At the last of the French and Indian Wars a British general, noting the rustic, homespun clothing of the colonials, named them, "Yankee Doodles." Many army songs were composed with this title.

Most famous was "Yankee Doodle Dandy," a war song of the Revolution with its twenty verses. Another was "The Riflemen at the Battle of Bennington," who won the fight under John Stark.

The war song in the War of 1812 was "The Star Spangled Banner," with its tune adapted from an old drinking melody.

Singing schools were organized and also choirs for the meetinghouses. A so-called choir stall was arranged at the front of the rear balcony with a small platform for the leader who used a tuning fork. This was a small, steel, two-tined instrument. The tines vibrated to the key of middle C or G usually, and the leader hummed the first note of the tune.

When denominations erected their churches, the choir seats were often in a balcony, over the vestibule, facing the pulpit. During the singing the audience rose and turned to face the choir. The bass viol was the first instrument that was allowed to be played in a Sabbath service.

In the first years of the nineteenth century, musical societies were organized in the Connecticut and Merrimack valleys called county sings. Groups of singers in the towns from Concord to Littleton paid experienced teachers to train them to read music and sing a new tune by sight.

Dr. Lowell Mason, who wrote or adapted the music for many sacred songs, became a teacher in 1887. He never allowed the words to be used until the notes were mastered.

Annual festivals were held at Bethlehem after the railroad was constructed. During several days programs of oratorios were given, such as Handel's *Messiah, Elijah,* and *Queen Esther.*

In the middle of the century the Estey Organ Company manufactured instruments for churches and hundreds of families bought them for their living rooms. Social gatherings sang "The Old Oaken Bucket" and the southern songs of Stephen Foster and the English and Scotch songs of Bobby Burns.

It is claimed that the soldiers sang the Civil War down. Both Southern and Northern men sang "The Battle Hymn of the Republic," "Tramp, Tramp," and "Marching Through Georgia."

When the army rejected Walter Kittredge of Merrimack, he wrote, "Tenting Tonight," still famous in New Hampshire. He was a troubadour who traveled from town to town entertaining with programs while he played his organ for accompaniment.

Choirs in the churches contributed to the study of religious compositions. The collection of songs, "The Gospel Hymns," were used at the Christian Endeavor Societies by many young people.

The schools employed trained musicians and concerts by high schools offered programs of modern compositions. Cantatas were frequently performed.

Lecture courses with programs supplied by agencies in Boston brought violinists and soloists from the Metropolitan Opera in New York.

The Victrola spread records of the finest singers and instrumentalists into thousands of homes and schools. Radio became popular about 1940 and a new type of music was introduced rapidly.

Today TV has attracted the attention of all ages—but the robins will always return in the spring. Their spring serenades are nature's contribution to the music of New Hampshire.

THREE HUNDRED YEARS OF EDUCATION

The beginning of public schools in the colony of New Hampshire is legendary. Without doubt the King James Bible of 1610 was the first text book and it is believed that pebbles were the materials for number work.

Imported paper was expensive but a white pine board and a charred twig served for writing, and quilled pens, fashioned from the tail or wing feather of a sea gull, were in use. Sheets of birch bark provided practice paper for penmanship.

Soon after the two colonies united in 1641, a law was enacted by the General Court that every town that contained fifty families must provide a public school. Records prove that a male teacher from Massachusetts was employed in Dover and another in Exeter in 1642. About 1700, Portsmouth was building two new schoolhouses.

A very early text book was the *Horn Book,* now a museum piece, so named because its back binding was horn. In 1785 "An easy and pleasant guide to the Art of Reading" named *The New England Primer,* was published in Boston for B. Larkin of Cornhill, and became a universal text book.

It contained as a frontispiece a picture of George Washington. There was the alphabet with each letter illustrated by a picture; poems, and the shorter catechism which was a long list of questions and answers beginning with, "What is the chief end of man?" and the answer, "Man's chief end is to glorify God and enjoy Him forever."

Every child was supposed to commit this catechism to memory. In the early towns that were granted after 1720, usually the minister taught catechism classes and reading and writing.

By law, school taxes built schoolhouses and later the towns merged into neighborhood districts. The town employed one teacher, a man who divided his time in proportion to the number of weeks that the taxes demanded. Later, women teachers served in spring and fall terms for the smaller pupils and a long winter term for teenaged boys and girls was taught by a husky man, often a student from Dartmouth.

Many a grandfather of today recalls tales that his grandfather related about how he assisted in scuffles to "carry out the teacher."

After the Revolution, higher branches were desired. In 1783 the wealthy Phillips family of Exeter founded Phillips Exeter Academy for boys. New Ipswich began an academy in 1789, later named Appleton Academy. Atkinson and Derry in 1790 and Haverhill and Gilmanton in 1794 were followed by twenty-five academies, several being co-educational.

When a bill was introduced into the legislature for an appropriation for higher branches, an aged man was heard to remark, "In our state we hain't believed much in edicating women." Not so in New Hampshire! Both girls and boys were legally admitted to public schools and several academies were opened for girls.

About 1875 high schools were established in the cities and larger towns and in 1870 the Plymouth State Normal School opened with one-year courses for experienced teachers and a two-year course for other pupils, both male and female.

By act of the legislature a department of education was established with a commissioner and several deputies who soon elevated the standards for teachers by demanding examinations in the common school subjects before a certificate of teaching was granted.

In 1910 eight hundred small rural schools were scattered over the state, all controlled by town school boards. The remarkable commissioner, Henry C. Morrison, who was soon called to become the superintendent of schools in Chicago, began to inspect these small schools. He found the buildings dilapidated, unsanitary, and the classes taught by inexperienced young women.

A law was enacted that permitted school taxes to be used to employ experienced educators for supervision of all schools.

Gradually, as bus service became available, rural schools disappeared. A law provided that, in towns where high school privileges did not exist, qualified students were permitted to attend a high school of their choice and the taxes of the town paid the tuitions.

Trained teachers were in demand and a second normal school was founded at Keene and the state university of New Hampshire opened at Durham. Today the three institutions are under the control of one board of trustees with the two normal schools now state colleges with power to grant both bachelor's and master's degrees.

The early academies are now, in some cases, junior colleges. Vocational courses are offered in all high schools and institutions that offer specialized vocational training are established in all sections of the state.

High schools are consolidating and multimillion dollar school buildings with modern equipment, classrooms, libraries, science departments, theaters, music rooms, and cafeterias should be inspected by all citizen taxpayers to complete their education today.

PATCHWORK QUILTS

The word patchwork was coined in the eleventh century. The word was adopted by our great-grandmothers; the designs that they created with scraps of cotton prints were an art form requiring great skill.

The hand-carved four-poster or canopy bedsteads were the pride of housewives. Instead of the metal springs of today, hemp rope was run through the holes in the frame, woven from side to side and top to bottom by one man pulling with his two hands on the rope while another man pressed down to stretch the rope to prevent sagging.

This foundation was covered with a mattress of straw or the inner husks of corn which was renewed every fall season. Above this was a feather bed of the down plucked from the breasts of geese when they were shedding their feathers, or the fine breast feathers of chickens.

Sheets were woven with fine linen warp and woolen woof. When these were covered with woolen blankets and an eight-foot comforter tucked around the three sides, our ancestors were warm during the cold winter nights even though the logs burned low in the fireplace.

After white cotton cloth was imported, our grandmothers dyed it for colors: indigo blue from the Carolinas, red seeds of cochineal of the Indies, yellow dandelion blossoms, green herbs, and brown bark.

From these colors they cut roses, tulips, or lilies, stems and leaves. These they sewed to squares of white cloth called applique. The squares were connected with strips of one color using thirty-six of the appliqued squares for a cover.

Quilting frames were four-to-ten-foot strips of pine, four inches wide and one inch thick with holes near one edge through which long needles threaded with twine were thrust to fasten the lining firmly on the four sides. The lining was usually an eight-foot square of cloth of one color. This was padded with cotton batting or worn blankets and then covered with the appliqued squares. Now all was ready for the quilting bee. A group of friends would be invited for a day of quilting or tacking—with the expectation of a bountiful dinner consisting of the recipes for which the hostess considered herself famous.

Quilting was the sewing through the three layers with long needles threaded with linen. The stitches might be in concentric circles, diagonals, or squares, with the lines an inch apart. Tacking was done with needles threaded with cotton twine. The needle was thrust down and then up through the three layers and then the ends were tied into a strong knot and cut about an inch in length.

Perhaps the workers arrived in an ox cart. Then the husbands would be invited for a hearty supper, the couples returning home by lantern light. Such was neighborhood sociability two centuries ago.

A century and a half ago cotton cloth of varied colors, called calico, was imported from Calcutta, India, for women's dresses. Every scrap left after cutting these garments was saved for patchwork. Fifty years later, the cotton mills in New England discovered the method of transferring designs in colors to white yard goods, prints, and patchwork became the pastime for all ages.

Women displayed their artistic skill by designing patterns for blocks composed of squares, rectangles, triangles, and diamonds in alternating light and dark prints, to which they assigned names such as star flower, Job's patience, or grandmother's garden.

Maidens began to sew "bride's quilts" of light prints that were quilted in varied stitches. Quaker women were expert in needlecraft. Their bride's quilts were white with embossed designs that required several years to create. They are now found in museums.

The log cabin pattern, popular when Harrison ran for president, was composed of narrow strips to represent logs. A popular pattern was hexagons about an inch in diameter arranged in light and dark designs called snowball and rose.

Crazy quilts were silk and velvety scraps fastened to a lining with fancy stitches of embroidery thread.

Museums display quilts of unusual designs. The sunburst is an allover pattern made of small diamonds shaded from a pale yellow center through tints of yellow to orange into reds sewed in concentric circles. One might search several years to find the colors of prints to represent a sunset.

Hidden away in trunks in attics or spread across the foot of a bed in a colonial home are specimens of grandmother's patchwork in intricate designs and combinations of color which prove the artistic skill of the housewives of past centuries.

JOHN GREENLEAF WHITTIER

A century ago the poet John Greenleaf Whittier was the popular author in the homes and schools in New Hampshire. He himself enjoyed many summers at Hampton Beach and in Plymouth, Campton, and Ossipee.

The poet was born on December 17, 1807, in the homestead that his great-great-grandfather Thomas built in 1688 at Haverhill, Massachusetts, in the East Parish.

When a "barefoot boy," he attended school in the "old schoolhouse by the road," milked seven cows, and worked in the fields. He began to write poems but hid them in the attic because his Quaker father disapproved of his compositions.

Sister Elizabeth discovered the poems and marked one "W" and sent it to William Lloyd Garrison, the editor of the *Emancipator,* an antislavery newspaper. Mr. Garrison discovered the poet and visited his home to urge his father to give more education to the young author.

John Whittier said "No!" A man could not earn a living writing poetry. However, an academy was opened in Haverhill in 1827 where the young poet attended several terms. His mother was a cultured Quaker and the library at the homestead contained classics that the boy read, together with books that were exchanged with other families.

He entered politics and was elected to the Massachusetts

legislature. He joined the antislavery party and wrote both prose and poetry for the cause. His introduction into New Hampshire was suddenly dangerous.

Mr. Whittier became acquainted with Nathaniel Rogers of Plymouth, New Hampshire, a prominent antislavery leader and a prosperous lawyer. In company with George Thompson of England, an eloquent lecturer against slavery, Mr. Whittier drove to visit Mr. Rogers in Plymouth. They stopped in Concord where Mr. Thompson was to lecture in the court house. Mistaking him for George Thompson, a mob of Southern sympathizers attacked Whittier with rotten eggs and stones. They followed with muskets and a cannon.

Fearing the house would be blown down, the two men, Whittier and Thompson, went to the stable, harnessed their horse and so rapidly rushed from the gate that the mob could not stop them.

Mr. Rogers sold his beautiful home in Plymouth to become, for about ten years, the editor of the *Herald of Freedom*, a newspaper in Concord. When he became ill, he purchased a farm in Plymouth where Mr. Whittier often boarded. Because a high ledge was close to the house they named the place "Undercliff"—and so it is called today.

In Campton Lower Village is a homestead where Mr. Whittier boarded during several summers. An aged citizen recalled that Whittier and the poet, Lucy Larcom, became friends there.

After the close of the Civil War in 1866, the poem *Snow-Bound* was written for which the publishers paid $10,000, much to the surprise of the author. The following year the collection of *The Tent on the Beach* was read to Mr. Ticknor, the publisher at Hampton Beach.

In later years, Ossipee's Whittier Inn was the summer home of the poet. A member of the well-known Lord family of Ossipee told me that when a child she often watched Mr. Whittier walking about the woods or sitting under a tree busily writing.

In 1833, after the death of his father, Mr. Whittier and his mother, sister Elizabeth, and an aunt sold the homestead and purchased the home in Amesbury near the Quaker meetinghouse.

About 1890 my chum at school enjoyed weekends with her relative who was the housekeeper at Amesbury. She said the aged poet always greeted her with a smile in the mornings. He lived in his loved garden or his well-filled library during his last years.

In North Hampton, New Hampshire, the poet died at his favorite cottage on September 7, 1892. The famous Hutchinson family of singers, antislavery friends, sang at his funeral. Several favorite hymns are from his poems, "Our Master" and "The Brewing of Soma," are often heard in church services today. Pupils in junior high schools read the poem *Barbara Frietchie.*

On October 12, 1892, the first Columbus Day, I visited my grandmother in the East Parish of Haverhill. My father was born there in 1849. His father died in 1852 and the small boy lived on Corliss Hill above the Whittier homestead with his aunt Mrs. Israel Ela.

In 1892 Monroe and Amelia Ela were the custodians of the Whittier homestead where Grandmother and I were entertained at evening tea. We used the blue and white Staffordshire tea cups and talked before the old fireplace while we learned about the many heirlooms that are preserved from the days of *Snow-Bound.*

Years later I visited the Whittier home in Amesbury now owned by The Whittier Home Association and preserved as in 1892. Grandmother Martha Ann (Foss) Clough was living in the square, brick Dustin House near Monument Square in Haverhill.

THE SAINT-GAUDENS MEMORIAL

New Hampshire is proud of the Saint-Gaudens Memorial in Cornish which is the final residence of the famous sculptor, Augustus Saint-Gaudens. This is now a national historic site, maintained by the National Parks Service.

Bertram Saint-Gaudens, the father of Augustus, was born in the hill village of Aspet in France. He became a shoemaker, joined a shoemakers guild, and traveled across France, to London, and Dublin, Ireland, making shoes all the way.

In a shoe shop in Dublin he saw a pretty Irish girl named Mary McGuiness, married her in three months—and they made shoes for seven years, during which time two boys died before Augustus was born on March 1, 1848.

The famine that raged in Dublin caused the three to board a sailing ship and in six weeks they landed in Boston. Bertram went to New York City, found a room there in a poverty street, and hung out his sign, "French Ladies Boots and Shoes." Soon he was so busy that he sent for Mary and Augustus.

They earned their living making shoes, changing their home to better locations as prosperity permitted, for their three boys and a girl. Augustus played with street gangs, learning to run when the fights became more than he could handle. He was allowed some schooling.

At the age of thirteen, his father told him that he must go to work and asked him what he would choose to do. He replied that he wished to become an artist. He was apprenticed to a cameo cutter but his father collected his wages.

Augustus worked skillfully at his lathe in the daytime and attended art classes at the free Cooper Union in the evenings, learning to draw and to paint. He transferred to the Academy of Design where his studies prepared him for his ambition to become a sculptor.

When he was nineteen, friends at the academy planned to attend an exhibit in Paris. His father asked him if he wished to go to Paris. To his astonishment the money was supplied from his wages that his mother had saved, together with 100 gold francs, for a trip to Aspet, his father's birthplace.

In Paris he boarded with a relative while he waited nine months for admission to the École des Beaux Arts. He learned the essentials for his art as a sculptor and earned his living with his cameo lathe. After three years, war in France caused him to move to Rome. He continued his studies while drawing portraits and making busts of daughters of wealthy Americans. He also designed a figure of Hiawatha in marble and another called *Silence* that he sold to Americans.

He learned that a statue of Admiral Farragut was planned in New York, and he returned home unannounced with the hope that he might obtain the commission for this monument. While at home, he became acquainted with a rising firm of architects, McKim, Meade and White, who were most helpful in his future career.

He returned to Rome for more study and became acquainted with a young painter, Miss Augusta Homer of Roxbury, Massachusetts. He married her after he had received the commission for the Admiral Farragut statue, and returned to New York to reside.

The Farragut monument in New York brought him fame and commissions for the Puritan monument in Springfield, Massachusetts, and the Shaw Memorial that stands before the State House in Boston.

Saint-Gaudens worked patiently, producing small models for the approval of commissioners, changing and enlarging them until they were accepted. He worked twelve years before the Shaw Memorial was unveiled, the same time as his Standing Lincoln.

His desire was to do a figure of Lincoln. When a lad he saw Lincoln in New York, and while Lincoln's body lay in state, the boy passed by his bier twice. Finally he made the Standing Lincoln and the Sitting Lincoln, both for Chicago. The latter was the model for the Lincoln Memorial in Washington by Daniel Chester French, done after Saint-Gaudens died.

In 1885 a wealthy friend purchased a summer home in Cornish, New Hampshire, and offered Saint-Gaudens an old brick house with a large barn and acres of land for $500. The barn was a good studio. This sculptor had the ability to see in a mass of clay the finished work he was creating.

The last statue was of Phillips Brooks, with the finger of

Christ upon his shoulder, beside Trinity Church in Boston.
The sculptor was so ill with cancer that he had to be carried
to work. It tells the spirit of the man, Saint-Gaudens.

He was generous to young artists, patient, understanding,
and patriotic. He loved his Cornish home, which he named
Aspet, where he is buried. He died there on August 3, 1907.

Mrs. Saint-Gaudens established the beautiful home with
its gardens and studio as a memorial to her husband soon after he died. The studio contains figures of his famous works
that everyone can study with pleasure.

THE ARTIST COLONY AT CORNISH

About the turn of the nineteenth century, many artists and
authors followed Augustus Saint-Gaudens to Cornish. The
many commissions that the sculptor received demanded assistants. His brother Louis and his wife, both skilled sculp-
tors, purchased several acres above Aspet and moved an
old church to this height for their home.

The beauty of the landscape, including Mount Ascutney
across the river in Vermont and the forested foothills above
the wide meadows, attracted a colony of skilled men and
women to Cornish as time passed.

The author Winston Churchill found a beautiful home on
the bank of the river where he produced his novel, *Richard
Carvell,* in 1899 and another best seller, *Coniston,* in 1908
which was a story of politics in New Hampshire seventy-five years ago. The Cornish Inn became a popular guest
house for Mr. Churchill's friends.

A cousin of Mrs. Saint-Gaudens, Sidney Homer, found a
farm house for his summer home. His wife was the opera
star, Madam Louise Homer. They renovated the corncrib
for a studio where Mrs. Homer practiced her arias with her
husband at the piano.

In later years the son, Homer Saint-Gaudens, married and
built his home near Aspet. There his wife, Carlotta, painted

her famous miniatures. Thus, a family group occupied the hillside.

The most famous of the artists was Maxfield Parish whom many of the older generation today will remember as the painter of the large posters that the state publicity bureau scattered widely. They featured landscapes done in the vivid autumn colors of red and yellow maples and the deep blue sky.

With his own hands, Mr. Parish built his home in a sheep pasture that overlooked the river. His swimming pool, unusual in Cornish, surrounded by a high stone wall, was a topic of conversation among the natives.

A doctor in Windsor, across the river, had recently purchased the first automobile in the vicinity. Mr. Parish displayed his lively sense of humor by drawing a picture of this machine on the outside of a package of his illustrations of cover designs for *Scribner's, Harper's,* or *Collier* magazines; this to influence the express agent to rush it to its destination.

His best known painting was of Old King Cole with his pipe and his bowl that hung above the bar in the Knickerbocker Hotel in New York. Mr. Parish and Sidney Homer were the life of the picnics and social gatherings of the colony.

Another summer cottage, hidden in a grove beside a brook, was the home of Mr. and Mrs. Sidney Cox. Two of his paintings, representing *The Arts* and *The Sciences,* hang in the Library of Congress. His most famous picture is *The Surprise* with a sudden attack of cupids against the heart of a young girl. His books and lectures were equally famous.

Mrs Cox's prize design on the cover of the *Woman's Home Companion* named *Feeding the Doves,* brought her nationwide fame. Her paintings of children were widely honored.

The cottage of Mr. Henry O. Walker was hidden on the edge of a ravine. He possessed an enviable reputation for his mural decorations, among them *Lyric Poetry,* in the Library of Congress, *The Landing of the Pilgrims,* in the State

House in Boston, and *The Wisdom of the Law*, at the Appellate Court House in New York.

Driving north toward the village of Plainfield one sees a square, white house where lived Mr. and Mrs. Henry Brown Fuller. Mr. Fuller was renowned for his painting *The Triumph of Truth over Error* for the Christian Science Society. Mrs. Fuller is in the highest rank of miniature artists. She held a bronze medal in Paris in 1900, a silver medal at Buffalo, and a gold one in Saint Louis in 1904.

Mr. Herbert Adams, a famous New England sculptor, resided in Cornish while working on a commission for a memorial of Senator MacMillan, a bust of Chief Justice Fuller, a portrait of Mrs. Billings of Woodstock, Vermont, and a commission for the courthouse in Cleveland, Ohio.

After the death of Augustus Saint-Gaudens, his brother Louis continued to work at Cornish upon the models of six heroic figures for the terminal station in Washington that were cut in granite at Northfield, Vermont.

Mrs. Annetta Saint-Gaudens, the wife of Louis, one of Augustus' most able assistants, completed commissions that remained after his death—such as the Phillips Brooks Memorial.

Another assistant, Miss Elsie Ward, made a statue of General George Rogers Clark, and a fountain for the Women's Christian Temperance Union, a group called *The Huguenots*. She also received a medal for her *Boy and a Girl*.

After Mrs. Saint-Gaudens died in 1926, the attraction to Cornish ceased and the colony ceased to exist. The village of Cornish became prosperous, with Saint-Gaudens Memorial at Aspet containing in its studio a collection of the models of the creations of the sculptor that attracts hundreds of visitors every summer.

THE MACDOWELL COLONY

The MacDowell Colony was constructed about fifty years

ago in Peterborough. Marian Nevins MacDowell, the widow
of the celebrated composer, Edward MacDowell, produced
a plan for a unique retreat where talented artists would live
in an undisturbed atmosphere, known as The MacDowell
Memorial Colony.

Edward MacDowell was born in New York City on December 18, 1861. A prosperous Scotch businessman and an
Irish wife were the parents of a son who became a musical
genius. He was nine years old when he was given his first
piano lesson.

Skilled musicians suggested that he go abroad for study
since all musicians were supposed to receive training in Europe. At fifteen he was accompanied by his mother to Paris.
After a year, he went to Germany. He studied at several
conservatories and he was both student and teacher at
Frankfurt.

His teacher suggested that he compose a personal piece
which he wrote in two weeks. The teacher was so impressed with this music he asked the composer to show his
work to Franz Liszt who said, "This young American will
be somebody."

A young pianist objected to a teacher only twenty years
of age, and he an American, since she had come all the way
to Europe to study. She changed her mind and married Edward MacDowell. They were in Germany one year, then
lived in Boston for eight years.

Mr. MacDowell was invited to Columbia University to or-
ganize a musical center which he hoped would soon offer
the equivalent of European study for young musicians.

After seven years of devoted effort, a new president of
Columbia, Nicholas Murray Butler, refused the funds for
the musical center, having other ambitions for the university. Disappointed and frustrated after a bitter controversy,
MacDowell's health failed and he resigned in 1904.

Mrs. MacDowell purchased a 100-acre, abandoned farm
in Peterborough where she took her sadly broken husband
to a quiet cabin to regain his health. But the collapse was
fatal and he died in 1907 at a hospital in New York. He

sleeps on a favorite hilltop on the farm in Peterborough.

From her years of acquaintance Mrs. MacDowell learned that many talented artists desired an undisturbed atmosphere for their creative work. She resolved to transform the farm into such a quiet retreat as a memorial to her husband.

The Mendelssohn Club of New York sent $30,000 to her and she "took to the road," as she remarked, to perform recitals, playing her husband's compositions as she interpreted them.

When she believed that funds were sufficient, she erected twenty-four studios scattered through her four hundred acres; not too isolated, yet undisturbed by the click of a typewriter or the din of a piano, each with a fireplace. Dormitories for sleeping quarters were erected, and a dining room, kitchen, a comfortable lounge, and a well-stocked library.

Breakfast and evening dinner were served daily. In a buggy with a skittish horse, Mrs. MacDowell carried firewood and noon lunch baskets to the studios. Each artist paid a small fee toward expenses. The MacDowell Association selected the applicants and provided funds.

That the experiment has been productive is proved from the twenty-three Pulitzer Prizes won by artists—many poets, three books by Edward Arlington Robinson, a novel by Willa Cather, a play by Thornton Wilder, a symphony, and concert numbers.

The colony was also a bird sanctuary with hermit thrushes singing day and evening, tame squirrels—even a hungry woodchuck became a pet.

A $35,000 mortgage became a burden to Mrs. MacDowell when illness troubled the concerts. The New Hampshire Federation of Women's Clubs came to her assistance with the story printed on a leaflet that brought in money. The mortgage was discharged in less than a year.

Mrs. MacDowell died at ninety-three in 1956. Then male direction took over, electricity and oil heat were installed everywhere. The memorial is now open year-round and fifty artists are provided for each year.

However, times are changing; prizes are won less frequently, expenses increase because of inflation, and the public seems to be less attracted to fine arts. Nevertheless, the colony is successful and the MacDowell Association in New York City still invites applications from talented people.

The Old Man of the Mountains, from a drawing by Isaac Sprague.

(8)

From Coos to the Sea

A HISTORY OF THE ISLES OF SHOALS

Only the cry of the seagulls or the splash of the waves against the shore disturbs the silence at the Isles of Shoals. The word shoals means shallow waters. Formerly called Shoal Islands, it has become the Isles of Shoals. Millions of years ago these rocky islands were the hard core of a chain of volcanic peaks that stood upon the Continental Shelf that has sunk 150 feet beneath the surface of the ocean.

The ice age of 10,000 years ago sheered off the tops of these mountains and left them to lie as dangerous reefs around the islands. The base of these nine islands was a volcano three miles in length.

The northern island is named Duck because, by that miracle of nature that causes water to seek its own level, a stream of fresh water rises to form a lake on this fifteen-acre isle where wild ducks rest on their spring and fall migrations.

Southward lies the largest of the group, ninety-five acres in extent, that bears the name of a fishing village in England, Appledore. Then Malaga (named by Spanish sailors), Smuttynose (because of its black point), and Cedar (where several cedar trees grew), lie in a semicircle.

Next is Star, a rock of thirty-nine acres that rises fifty-five feet above the waves. Finally Londoner and Seavey which become one island at very low tide.

To the east is White Island, surrounded by reefs that are so dangerous that the supply ship for the keepers of the light lands but twice a year. White Island Light stands ninety feet in height and flashes a yellow beam at stated intervals.

English fishermen were living on these islands when Captain John Smith discovered them in 1614. A fishing village of 300 families developed after a method of preserving fish was discovered. The fisher folk on Star and Appledore sold preserved fish for four times the price of fresh fish.

Pirates frequented the isles, Blackbeard and Captain Kidd among them. At least $100,000 of pirate gold has been discovered at the Isles and it is believed that more treasure lies around the rocky shores.

About 1756 Captain Haley built a house on Smuttynose and developed a windmill, gristmill, coopershop, and other buildings. While looking for rocks to build a seawall between Smuttynose and Malaga, he found several bars of pure silver that he sold for about $4,000. This permitted him to complete a wall to Cedar and have a safe harbor for small boats. His son carried on later.

Thomas Leighton, the son of a wealthy family in Portsmouth, loved the sea. In 1839 he bought Appledore, Malaga, Cedar, and Smuttynose. He had a wife, a daughter, Celia, and two sons, Cedric and Oscar. He became the keeper of White Island Light and lived there six years.

Celia was born in 1835 and her greatest pleasure was to help her mother care for the light while her father was absent from home. When of school age she went to Boston for several years.

Levi Thaxter came to the islands to begin the hotel business. He and Thomas Leighton opened a house on Smuttynose and in 1848 they erected the large hotel named Appledore House on that island. This became a favorite vacation resort for many musicians, poets, and authors.

When Celia was only fifteen years of age, she married Levi Thaxter. With their three children they lived in Boston. Levi was a traveler and with his sons he went to Florida while Celia cared for an invalid mother, meanwhile beginning to write the poems that brought fame in later years.

After the death of Levi, she lived at her cottage on Appledore writing her poems and cultivating her garden where she is now sleeping in her grave that is visited by many people.

In 1818 the Unitarian Association of Boston purchased Star Island where the Oceanic Hotel had been erected. There they developed their summer conferences, later joined by the Congregationalist group. Today these gatherings are crowded.

A visit to Star Island offers many attractions. The islanders built a chapel on the highest spot with the wood from a wrecked ship. This building burned in 1720 and another was erected which was torn down for fuel in the bitter winter of 1790. The present chapel was erected in 1800. A light has shone from its tower at night throughout the years.

There is a monument to Captain John Smith and another to the memory of Reverend John Tuck who served as minister from 1713 to 1732.

To stay a night on Star, to attend the quiet vesper service, to arise and watch the dawn light the fog with its colors, is an adventure of a lifetime.

EARLY SETTLERS
IN CRAWFORD NOTCH

Without doubt the first white man to travel Crawford Notch was Timothy Nash, an early settler in Lancaster before 1771. He was a hunter, for the fur trade was offering good prices.

While tracking a deer, the hunter strayed into unknown forest paths and into the vicinity of the present Crawford Hotel. Astonished by the many unknown mountain peaks, he climbed a tree for a wider view.

To the south he saw a deep valley shut in by high cliffs on either side. At his feet a small stream flowed down a narrow defile. Curiosity urged him to explore this valley. Cascades were leaping from the side of Mount Webster, joining the little stream to become a river.

On and on Timothy Nash traveled until he found settlements and finaly Portsmouth. There he told Governor John

Wentworth, Jr., about his surprising trip and advised that a road should be cut into the far north.

A bargain was made. If Nash could lead a horse over his trail, the governor would authorize a road. Thinking about several rough places, Timothy returned to Lancaster determined to win the bargain.

He enlisted the aid of Benjamin Sawyer and together they rigged a leather girdle around the body of a horse. Supplied with many ropes, they started with the horse for Portsmouth.

All went safely until they reached a ledge now called Sawyer's Rock near Bemis Station. Carefully they lowered the horse down the ledge and on they went to arrive before the door of the governor's house in Portsmouth with the horse.

True to his promise, a road was authorized but the Revolution caused Governor Wentworth to flee to England and the road was not completed until another twenty or more years. Later the two hunters discovered a clearing near the present Crawford Hotel that they named "Nash and Sawyer's Location." This is the site of the famous Fabyan Hotel and the junction of railroads in later years.

Eleazer Rosebrook, another stalwart hunter, from Grafton, Massachusetts, with his wife and baby daughter, arrived at Lancaster in 1772 looking for a grant along the Connecticut River. After a few months, and with two daughters, they walked, leading a cow, thirty miles north to Colebrook where they built a log cabin.

While Eleazer was hunting, Mrs. Rosebrook lived many days alone, often obliged to wade the river with her baby in her arms to lead the cow home after she had strayed to greener fields; always fearing that an Indian had entered the cabin where the older child was alone.

When the Revolution began, Eleazer took his family across the river to Guildhall to live alone in a cabin while he enlisted in the war. Frequently groups of intoxicated Coos Indians crowded into the cabin hoping to sell their furs. Mrs. Rosebrook often was obliged to push them out.

One day a drunken squaw sat motionless on the floor. Grasping her long hair, Mrs. Rosebrook dragged the squaw outside where she awoke. Seizing her tomahawk, she aimed it at Mrs. Rosebrook's head, only missing because the door closed.

Fearing what the Indians might do, a restless night followed. The next morning the sorry squaw came begging for forgiveness.

Such was the life of a pioneer wife. After 1790, Eleazer sold his farm and bought the Nash and Sawyer's Location, later named Fabyans. There he built a two-story house against a mound called the Giant's Grave, barns, and a grist and sawmill. In 1808 when the highway became the throughway to Portland and Portsmouth, Rosebrook Inn was opened and descendants have operated a Rosebrook Inn to the present day.

After Eleazer died of cancer, the property was inherited by his grandson, Ethan Allen Crawford, the son of Abel Crawford, another famous pioneer from Vermont. He cut the first footpath to the top of Mt. Washington and guided early tourists to the top.

Ethan Allen Crawford was named "The Pathfinder of the Notch." He blazed the eight-mile path to the top of Mt. Washington and later discovered a shorter path that is the line of the Cog Railway, now a century in age.

A tradition tells that the Giant's Grave was cursed by an Indian who waved a burning torch about his head while he shouted, "Let no white man take root here."

The day that Ethan's first child was born, fire consumed all of the buildings with the exception of one small shed. All were immediately rebuilt and again burned. Years later two Fabyan hotels on the same Giant's Grave have successively burned, probably because of lightning.

The first Crawford House was erected at the entrance of the Notch. Many famous guests were entertained and guided up the mountains, among them Daniel Webster. In his famous diary, Mr. Crawford wrote about the complaints of Mr. Webster because the mountain welcomed him with a snow squall.

Today a small inn bears the Rosebrook name; a trout

brook to the north is Nash Stream; and Sawyer's Rock by the Saco River, Crawford Notch, and the second Crawford House are constant reminders of these hardy pioneers of two centuries ago.

HAYES AND DOLLY COPP

Scores of families are pitching their tents for a vacation at the Dolly Copp Campground at the northern outlet of Pinkham Notch.

The pioneer settler at the northern settlement was Hayes Dodifer Copp who was born in Stowe, Maine, in 1804. He was fortunate to possess strength of body and ambition to own a farm. He had heard about meadows along the Peabody River on the other side of the Carter Range.

About the time the present state house was completed in 1825 Hayes asked the legislature for a grant of that valley promising he would pay for it as soon as he could raise crops there. The legislature granted his request.

At the age of twenty-four years he began to build his log cabin and in five years he owned his grant, log buildings for his home, and shelter for his horse and cow. Soon he owned a pig, sheep, and hens.

Meanwhile, when he rode down the Notch to Jackson for supplies he met blue-eyed, flaxen-haired Dolly Emery and lost his heart. Dolly, born in Bartlett, was an up-to-date maiden who visited the cities, attended the theater, and purchased shoes for she was proud of her tiny feet. As long as she lived, she wore fine shoes.

When the home was ready, Dolly promised to marry Hayes. On a chill day in November, 1831, they pledged their vows and started up the Notch on their wedding trip, with winter ahead.

Hayes had constructed a drag by trimming two saplings about twelve feet in length and fastened the small end to the stirrups of the saddle while the larger ends dragged along the trail.

A platform between the logs held household necessities and Dolly's haircloth-covered trunk which she had packed with her personal needs and the family heirlooms—a silver teapot and spoons, a gold-banded china tea set, and her wedding gifts.

Dolly rode the horse while Hayes walked beside her. This journey probably required one or two nights with a camp in the forest.

In the lonely Peabody Valley they developed a farm; Hayes with his deliberate habits, Dolly filled with creative energy.

They transplanted the wild apple trees and nourished them for a thrifty orchard. Swarms of wild bees were hived for honey. Dolly had learned to dip candles, to make soft soap, to card wool, spin it into yarn, and weave or knit it into cloth. She raised flax, shredded the fibers and spun them into linen thread on her flax wheel.

Four children were born: Jeremiah, Nathan, Sylvia, and Daniel. A framed house replaced the log cabin and an ell was added later. Abundant crops of grain and corn were raised.

Travelers came to admire the presidential peaks and Dolly opened the home for a tavern. She drew her table before the fireplace, covered it with her fringed, white linen cloth, arranged the gold-banded china, and served tea in the silver heirloom with slices of pink ham, hot corncake, honey, and apple butter. The price for food and lodging per night was seventy-five cents. This included a feather bed, linen sheets, and blue homespun blankets.

In 1852 stagecoaches were running between Gorham and Conway where the railroad had been constructed and the Glen House erected. Dolly became a gift shop hostess. Her apple butter, jam, fresh butter and cheese, linen and blue homespun woolens pleased many. Savings began to accumulate for this busy family.

When the season was favorable, Hayes raised tobacco. Dolly smoked a pipe as did many women of her period. It is reported that a barrel of tobacco was the first product to be shipped through Crawford Notch.

The children grew older. One winter day son Nat became lost while hunting and traveled hours across the Carter Range to safety. His father searched through the night with two neighbors and it was late into the next afternoon when he found Nat safe. Neither father or son ever fully recovered from these twenty-six hours of winter suffering.

Nat married and lived in Littleton; Daniel married one of the city boarders and went to live in Ohio; Sylvia married and lived in Auburn, Maine, and Jerry became a wanderer for years.

In her old age, Dolly became restless with the mountain environment. When Sylvia offered a home to her parents, Dolly was eager to accept, but Hayes refused to live in a town.

Then this aged couple quietly agreed to divide their family savings equally between them. Hayes went back to his childhood home and Dolly to Auburn. Both exchanged visits occasionally.

Dolly said, "Hayes is well enough. But fifty years is enough for any woman to live with any man."

In 1885 Nat sold the farm and the Copp family was gone from the valley. Today the Dolly Copp Campground in the National Forest is a vacation spot for thousands of campers. Many enjoy a cold drink at Dolly Copp's spring and ask, "Who was Dolly Copp?"

NAMING THE PEAKS
OF THE WHITE MOUNTAINS

The name Wambed Mentha (White Mountains) originated with the Abanaki Indians. While the red men worshipped the Great Spirit, they also feared the evil spirit, Manitou, the white man's devil.

Manitou dwelt upon the summit of Mount Washington and no Indian climbed among the clouds at the summit because the evil spirit would kill anyone who invaded his kingdom.

Whether Adino N. Brackett, John N. Wheeler, Charles J. Stuart, Noyes S. Dennison, and Samuel A. Pearson were authorized by the legislature to name the peaks is unknown to me, but the fact that they invited Phillip Carrigan, then a famous designer of maps of New Hampshire, indicates that a record of this climb may exist.

Ethan Allen Crawford was the guide. He was known as "Giant of the Hills," being nearly seven feet tall. If any of his guests gave out he would bring them down the mountain on his back.

They spent the night of July 30, 1820, at a camp three miles from the Notch Road and in the morning set out on the intended expedition. They came to a pond of clear water about one mile from the summit of Mount Washington. Here they spent some time enjoying the delicious water, then proceeded to the summit.

They gave names to the peaks and drank healths of "Black Betts" with rousing cheers in honor of the great names they gave them. Their toasts were punctuated with considerable hilarity owing to frequent libations of Black Betts. On their descent they saw a beautiful sheet of water which they named Blue Pond (now known as the Lake of the Clouds).

Copious drinks of Blue Pond water with Black Betts began to have a weakening effect upon the knees of one of the party. Locomotion was no longer possible and Ethan was burdened with a back load of mortality weighing two hundred pounds all the way down the Ammonoosuc Valley.

Arriving at camp Ethan was so exhausted that after unloading his burden, he prostrated himself on the ground and told his party they would have to take care of themselves for the night. Thus the White Mountain peaks were named.

Apparently the Crawford daughters who wrote the diaries from which this story is taken were intending to record the exploits of Ethan Allen Crawford in this expedition rather than the naming of the peaks, since they mention only Mount Washington in their story.

The names were given in honor of the heights of the peaks rather than their position in the range: Washington, Adams, Jefferson, Madison, and Monroe.

Years later a lower peak of Mount Adams was named for his son, John Quincy Adams, who was president in 1825.

Two peaks in the Franconia Range honor presidents, Lincoln and Garfield. An assassin attempted to kill President Garfield. He was brought to a cottage on the side of the mountain with the hope that the mountain air would speed his recovery. After his death in 1881 the mountain was named in his honor.

A lower peak to the west of Mount Washington bears the name of President Pierce (but usually called Clinton), and the legislature of 1969 changed the name of the small peak in the same vicinity from Mount Pleasant to Mount Eisenhower.

Two peaks in Lincoln are called Big and Little Coolidge, but they honored a family by this name long before Calvin Coolidge became a president.

(Parts of this story were adapted from the diaries of Placentia Crawford Wheeler and Hattie B. Crawford.)

FRANCONIA NOTCH, MECCA FOR TOURISTS

Before 1790 apparently, Franconia Notch was almost unknown. A petition by the citizens of the towns of Lisbon, Littleton, and Franconia was sent to the legislature of 1793 for a road through the Notch to begin at Plymouth and go on to Woodstock. Nothing came of this request and it was repeated five years later.

Certainly a road was cut through the Notch, because a tale is repeated about a young lad who was sent with an important message to his father who was at a road camp in Franconia Notch. When overtaken by a blinding tempest, and not finding the path, the lad remembered that a horse will go instinctively to other horses, so he gave his horse its head and arrived safely at the camp.

Before 1825 a footpath had been cut to the top of Great Haystack Mountain. During that summer a party which included ladies and a ten-year-old girl climbed the mountain to change its name to Mount Lafayette. The local story is that Mrs. Isaac Smith, the wife of the president of the Franconia Iron Works, ascended the mountain wearing a green silk gown and a leghorn hat trimmed with white ribbon. She probably broke a bottle of wine on the ledge of the summit and named the peak for the famous French general of the Revolution who had returned to New England to be present at the dedication of the Bunker Hill Monument at Charlestown, Massachusetts.

In August of 1826 there occurred the disastrous storm and landslide that killed the Willey family in Crawford Notch. This same tempest so destroyed the road in Franconia that it was not passable until the following November.

Not until 1835 was a stage wagon transporting tourists to the Flume and the famous Old Man of the Mountain. The accommodations for travelers was a rude roadhouse near the Flume named the Knight's Tavern.

The first hotel in the Notch was opened in 1835 by E.J. Giff called the Lafayette House that stood on the site of the present Tramway Station. Before 1848 the first Flume House rivaled Knight's Tavern.

In 1849 Richard Taft, a native of Barre, Vermont, purchased both of these hotels. Travelers were entertained at $1.50 per day. A branch of the railroad arrived in Plymouth in 1850 and regular stage lines brought guests who remained a month or throughout the summer.

Mr. Taft built the first Profile House in 1858. Two years later he employed a young lad named Charles Greenleaf, who together with Richard Taft, became the popular managers of summer hotels. Mr. Greenleaf succeeded Mr. Taft at the Profile and in later years was the manager of the Vendome Hotel in Boston.

Business increased to demand that the Profile House be

enlarged in 1866 and again in 1872.

In the late 1850s another rival was erected on the town line between Franconia and Lincoln, the Mount Lafayette House. A path to the top of Mount Lafayette was made passable for horses but this trail was abandoned after this hotel fell to the menace of fire in 1861 and was not rebuilt.

The first Flume House also burned in 1871 and was immediately rebuilt, a long, two-story building. Fire consumed this hotel in 1918 and the present Tea House was erected the following year on the opposite side of the highway.

The original Profile Hotel was replaced in 1900 by an up-to-date, three-story hotel that catered to a wealthy clientele. The branch line of the Pemigewasset Railroad was extended to Lincoln and until automobiles became available, the Concord Coach transported guests over the narrow, dusty road through the Notch to the hotel.

When golf became the popular summer sport, the Knickerbocker Golf Club opened a course on the side of the highway toward Bethlehem, and the Profile House became a popular house for its members. On the ridge behind the hotel a line of summer cottages was popular with artists and opera singers.

In 1923 while guests were at lunch a fire, supposedly of incendiary origin, consumed the entire complex. Guests rushed to save their valuables—only to discover that their valuables had been stolen. On the following day a hotel at Jackson was burned and another at Squam Lake in Holderness the next day. These were under like circumstances and seemed to indicate the work of a gang of thieves.

The Profile Hotel was not rebuilt. Bethlehem had already become a village of hotels. Sugar Hill and Bretton Woods supplied many new hostels, while hard-surfaced highways brought tourists in their automobiles who preferred the tourist homes and later the motels.

Franconia Notch became the property of the state of New Hampshire in 1925.

SYLVESTER MARSH
AND THE COG RAILWAY

The name of Sylvester Marsh should be remembered with highest admiration because his mechanical genius and initiative made it possible to complete the cog railway to the summit of Mount Washington in 1869.

Toward the close of the eighteenth century, John Marsh and his wife and several children traveled from a small hamlet not far from Rhode Island Sound to Campton, New Hampshire, seeking a home in the new township.

They purchased a forested meadow on the east bank of the Pemigewasset River and raised a family of eleven children. The ninth, named Sylvester, was born on September 30, 1803.

In the rural school he read every book he saw, especially eager for information about machinery. He learned to do his share on the farm, always tinkering with the farm tools until he was twenty-one.

In the spring of 1823 he walked forty miles to Concord in a day; to Amoskeag the second day; and to Boston the third. He stayed the first night in Boston at the best hotel for the price of one dollar.

He found work on a farm in Newton at twelve dollars per month but returned to Campton in the fall. In 1826 he was again in Boston selling meat at a stall in the Quincy Market. He soon went to Ashtabula, Ohio, and began to sell meat to Boston and New York by the Erie Canal route.

In 1833 he was in Chicago, then a village of 300 people, and he began to sell meat to the inhabitants of the village and to the soldiers at Fort Dearborn. He initiated the meat packing business of Chicago. Always seeking for methods to relieve human labor, he invented many tools to be used in this business.

Later he added grain to his enterprises and found a process for dried meal called Marsh's Caloric Dried Meal that became an article of commerce in markets far and wide. Within eighteen years he accumulated a fortune that permitted him to retire to a home in Jamaica Plain, Massachusetts.

In 1844 Mr. Marsh married Miss Charlotte D. Bates and a son and daughter were born before Mrs. Marsh died in 1852. He later married Miss Cornelia Hoyt and three daughters were added to his family.

In company with a clergyman he climbed Mount Washington one August day. Delayed by a storm, they did not arrive at the summit until late in the evening. Mr. Marsh said there should be a railroad up the mountain and never forgot his idea.

Apparently he discussed his plans with an inventor of knitting machinery, Mr. Aiken, from Franklin, New Hampshire. His great-granddaughter long afterward said that Mr. Aiken suggested the cog rail and made a model of his plan.

Mr. Marsh, however, devised his own model and applied to the legislature in New Hampshire for a charter to build a railroad to the summit of Mount Washington. The lawmakers ridiculed the idea, one man suggesting a charter to the moon. Nevertheless, a charter was granted in 1858 to erect a railroad on the northwest side of the mountain.

Mr. Marsh began to invent an engine that would maintain a speed of three miles per hour either up or down the mountain, but the Civil War interrupted the work, and he returned to Chicago where he produced additional machines for the meat packing business. In 1864 he removed to Littleton, New Hampshire, and continued to invent parts for his engine and to plan the track.

With his son he surveyed the route and determined the number of feet of grade to the mile the railroad must rise, and a skilled highway engineer confirmed their figures. He established a base station and erected several buildings for the workmen.

The road between Littleton and the base station was so rough that he built his engine in parts and assembled it in a blacksmith shop at the base. A sawmill cut the timbers for the ties that were necessary to brace the middle cog rail of the track up the mountain.

Mr. Marsh constructed a complete model of his inclined track and train which he ran in his office in Littleton. This convinced the officials of the New York and Boston railroads that his plan did work and they invested their money in the construction.

During five years Mr. Marsh advanced $30,000, for which he received no remuneration, and supervised the work until July 3, 1869, when the first train climbed to the summit amid the great excitement of the owners of the road and newspaper reporters.

Although Mr. Marsh did not assume authority for the management of the road, he acted as president of the Mount Washington Steam Railroad Company for a few years, but he removed to reside in Concord where he died on December 30, 1884.

The *Granite Monthly Magazine* of 1885 stated: "Mr. Marsh was a public spirited citizen, fond of his home and family, a devout Christian and scrupulous in every business transaction.

"He was a typical New Englander, a founder of institutions, a promoter of every enterprise beneficial to society."

TOURISM—OLD STYLE

To recall horse and buggy days of eighty years ago seems like a fairy tale. At the close of the nineteenth century, six miles per hour was considered a rapid pace for a good horse to travel.

One sunny day in September, 1896, this writer was startled by three loud trumpet blasts. Along a dusty road in Vermont appeared a rider upon a bay horse wearing a dark blue uniform with brass buttons, sounding a brass trumpet that resembled pictures of Gabriel's. An automobile was approaching.

Vermont required that the driver of a horseless vehicle should announce his vehicle on the highway to permit approaching teams to control their horses and avoid accidents.

Soon the exhaust of an engine was heard and a small machine appeared resembling a horseless buggy. The driver steered by a cane in his hand. The machine moved about ten miles per hour. In a few minutes from the other direction came a horse and buggy, the driver grasping the reins tightly to check the speed of his frightened animal.

Five years later Fords and Cadillacs were frequently on the streets and horses became less afraid. A neighbor offered rides on Sunday afternoons. When the inexperienced driver attempted to climb to our favorite view, the passengers pushed to arrive at the summit.

The surface of the highways was uneven and the tires were hard rubber which often bounced the heads of the passengers against the car's top if the speed was over twenty miles per hour.

Usually in fair weather the tops were folded like a fan behind the rear seat. The men wore caps pressed firmly over their foreheads. Women tied yards of veils over their hats and everybody protected themselves with long linen dusters.

Soon the hard rubber tires were replaced by inflated tubes that frequently became flat from the stones and rough surface of the highways. Extra tires and sometimes wheels with new tires were under every hood. It was customary to courteously offer assistance if a car overtook another in trouble.

If a vacant seat were available, a pedestrian was offered a ride without thought of danger, and many a student thumbed his way back and forth to college over the weekend.

The state highway system began in 1905. Roads were widened and dangerous curves straightened. About 1915 oil was sprayed to lay the dust that concealed cars as they passed one another.

Gasoline taxes provided hard-surfaced state highways within a few years—made of blocks of concrete in the beginning. The increase in improvement in road machinery was rapid and new materials for hard surfaces also appeared.

The tourists began to demand accommodations for over-night stops. First in the villages, signs appeared "Tourists, $1 per night," then along the farms.

Scores of housewives were surprised to find their purses filling with fifty to one hundred dollars during the summer months. Breakfasts of bacon and eggs, hot muffins or griddle cakes and maple syrup, and fresh doughnuts added a dime to the usual price of fifty cents—believe it or not.

The tourists were surprised to sleep on goosefeathered beds with straw mattresses beneath these. The handmade quilts and woven counterpanes were attracting customers, thus winter quilting bees became popular at the Ladies Aid in the rural churches or the Grange.

Cabin colonies began to appear near the scenic spots. The Indian Head was one of the first experiments at one dollar per person. A forest fire had revealed this profile un-expectedly.

Peckett's on Sugar Hill opened for winter guests. Two-seated sleighs met the trains at Littleton with actual buffalo robes for protection against the winter cold. Guests wore long fur coats of coonskin and even mink.

Snowshoe hikes to the Old Man view in Franconia Notch and maple sugar parties on the snowdrifts were attractions about 1915.

The state acquired Franconia Notch in 1925 and the tram-way was erected within a few years. College students began to ski and New Hampshire enjoyed a four season attraction that has increased to become a million dollar business, un-imagined a half century ago.

As one remembers, truly a fairy tale is revealed today when superhighways are open the year around from Coos to the sea. Millions of travelers are finding pleasure in all seasons in beautiful New Hampshire.

JEAN LOUIS AGASSIZ
ROAMS THE NORTH COUNTRY

On May 28, 1807, Jean Louis Agassiz was born in the Swiss village of Montier, the son of the minister. He attended the village schools and attained a brilliant record that earned for him scholarships in the Swiss University.

Fascinated by the crocus that pushes through the melting snow in April, bursting into blooms of many colors in the Swiss spring, young Agassiz began the study of botany.

While hunting the flora, he discovered the fossils of many varieties of fish and turned to identify these, writing many scientific articles about them.

While he was occupied in his writings, an experienced geologist told him about discoveries of the marks that glaciers had left as they had melted over the entire countryside.

Agassiz began to study this theory of a previous ice age and became so excited that he dropped his writing about the fossils.

With a skilled guide he carried timbers to build a shelter on a glacier where they lived several summers. Agassiz began to lecture about the discoveries he was finding about former ice ages.

The publisher of the articles about fossils began to complain so Agassiz returned to this uncompleted work for several years.

With this finished, the glaciers received his entire attention. His guide and he returned to the hut. To his astonishment, it had disappeared. The guide said to look below.

They scrambled down the ice to discover that the hut was still whole and the fact dawned upon the surprised scientist that a glacier slides down the slope as it melts at its base.

After years of study, Agassiz decided to explore a deep crevice and he took the risk. Timbers were slid across the wide crevasse and ropes attached. Suspended by these ropes he descended between long icicles until he plunged into a chilling stream. Fortunately the guides caught his signals before he perished.

The final task in Switzerland was to climb the ice covered peak of Mount Jungfrau, 13,670 feet in height. With a group of experienced guides he started before dawn and arrived at the base at sunrise. To climb the last slope they cut 700 footholds in the glacier. At the top, only one man had space to stand, yet time was allowed for each hardy climber to view the hundreds of miles of gleaming landscape before descending the 700 steps.

The lectures on the theories about ice sheets were becoming famous in America. When he was about forty-five years of age, Agassiz received an invitation to join the department of geology at Harvard University at a tempting salary.

While still a young man, Agassiz had married a girl of distinguished family and they now had a family of several teen-aged children. Because her husband was obliged to be absent from home for many months, Mrs. Agassiz and the children were living at the home of her parents. She refused to remove to Cambridge, yet the invitation seemed too important to reject. He left Switzerland and it so happened that he never returned to his native land.

The story of his years of study of ice is too long to relate, first in New England, then across the continent, and even into the valley of the Amazon River. Discoveries proved that at least four ice sheets had covered the northern section of the earth, south from the North Pole to the fortieth parallel of latitude during the past 150,000 years.

Suddenly, Mrs. Agassiz died. Her husband was filled with remorse and for a time, because of his seeming neglect, further work became impossible. His eldest son arrived to comfort him and he recovered. This young man was then a scientist himself who made a distinguished record in America.

After traveling so widely, at the age of seventy years, Agassiz visited Bethlehem, New Hampshire, in 1870 to view the White Mountains. For six weeks he made his headquarters at the Sinclair Hotel, built in 1865.

He was surprised at the discoveries he made on the tops of the Presidential Range and in Tuckerman, Huntington, and Jefferson ravines. He visited the ravine on Moosilauke and the Agassiz Basin in Woodstock.

His last discovery was when he clambered from the cliff of the hill that is seen along the north side of Bethlehem's Main Street, now named Mount Agassiz.

At the east side of Mount Agassiz he found a rockfall of enormous boulders that had settled upon the ice sheet without shattering as the glacier melted. This was his final proof that ice sheets covered this region.

We wish that he had seen Lost River's potholes and the great boulder at Polar Caves in Rumney for additional proof.

Agassiz married a second wife who copied these records to preserve them in the archives of Harvard University.

Soon after his visit at Bethlehem, he suffered heart attacks and he died in 1873.

THE CAVERNS OF LOST RIVER

While the Great Stone Face in Franconia Notch is a most wonderful feature of the White Mountains, only a few miles to the west of the Old Man, in Kinsman's Notch, the caverns of Lost River are equally remarkable.

The late James W. Goldthwait, famous geologist of Dartmouth College, claimed that the Lost River Caverns are a rock-fall of a chain of potholes that a stream cut into a granite slope on Mount Kinsman 35,000 years ago, between the third and fourth ice age.

As the mile-deep glacier melted and slipped into Kinsman's Notch, it carried the potholes with it without breaking them. Now Lost River Brook flows above or below the potholes and emerges to the surface through the circle of an inverted pothole at the beautiful Paradise Falls.

About the period when the state was establishing the county seat of Grafton County at Haverhill in 1774, settlers were coming through Sandwich Notch to Peeling, now the town of Woodstock. They made a trail through Franconia Notch in 1803 and discovered the Old Man, and another up the Moosilauke Brook, past Lost River to Bungy, now Easton, in 1810, to Haverhill, the present Route 112.

Finally in 1840, a soldier of the War of 1812 by the name of Royal Jackman built his home on Mount Cilley and a sawmill on Jackman's Brook. He was a farmer, lumberman, and a member of the Advent denomination. His eldest son was named Royal C., Jr., and the youngest was Lyman.

One day in 1852 the two boys were hunting and fishing in the vicinity of Moosilauke Brook when Lyman suddenly disappeared. Fortunately Royal heard his call, for he had stepped upon a bank of moss that covered a cavern and was standing fifteen feet down in a waist-deep pool of water.

After the brother managed to rescue Lyman, they knelt in prayer to thank God that Lyman was alive. Thus Lost River was discovered.

Soon Royal married and resided away from New Hampshire for thirty years. Lyman enlisted in the Civil War in the famous Sixth Regiment. Then he married and lived in Concord where he organized one of the most successful insurance companies in New England.

When the fame of the Old Man brought tourists to the mountains, Isaac Fox erected the House of Seven Gables at North Woodstock and guided his guests on trips among the mountains.

One September day in 1874 he led a party of men and women, including Royal C. Jackman, on a camping trip to explore Lost River. At a certain spot Royal pointed to a hole and said, "There is the place where my brother discovered Lost River."

The name was fixed after a woman of this party sent an article to Boston and New York newspapers using the name that brought reporters to the caverns. Then the railroad came to Woodstock in 1890. This caused the tourist business to greatly increase.

Lost River became famous. In 1912 Mr. Edward W. Rollins, the brother of the governor, built the Rollina Shelter, a cottage with necessary facilities surrounded by picnic grounds with fireplaces. The state constructed an automobile highway to Lost River in 1915.

In 1908 the Society for the Protection of New Hampshire Forests acquired 150 acres which included Lost River. Then enthusiastic forester Philip W. Ayers began to plan. In 1911 he persuaded the New Hampshire Federation of Women's Clubs to contribute $625.45 for boardwalks and stairways through the caverns.

Crowds of tourists demanded better equipment. An administration building, lunch rooms, lounge, and business offices were added.

Mr. Ayers persuaded a skilled botanist to plan a wild garden that grew a collection of wild orchids. There are rare ferns such as the unusual walking fern and many specimens of the unique flora of the mountain region.

The trip through the potholes of Lost River is a new experience for the agile tourist whether one chooses to scramble through the so-called Lemon Squeezer or to take the path around it.

For the scientist, Lost River proves the words of Shakespeare:

"And this our life, exempt from public haunts.
Finds tongues in trees, books in the running brooks
Sermons in stones, and good in everything."

THE POLAR CAVES IN RUMNEY

In addition to the Old Man of the Mountain and the potholes at Lost River, a third unique rock-fall, called Polar Caves, is located at the southern boundary line between Rumney and Plymouth on Route 25.

In the last record that Louis Agassiz wrote, he tells about the glaciers of the White Mountains that did not disappear until several hundred years after the ice sheet withdrew into Canada 10,000 years ago.

When the glacier in the deep ravine on the west side of Moosilauke gradually melted and slipped down the Baker River Valley, it strewed the foothills of the Rattlesnake Range with unusually large boulders. The glacier made Groton Hollow and covered the cliff that the settlers named Clark Hill, now named Haycock Mountain. The frost cracked large boulders off this cliff that now lie in a jumbled position, creating Polar Caves.

Finally, frost separated the largest boulder known on this continent, and perhaps in the world, off Haycock Mountain. It slipped upon the glacier without breaking and gradually settled at the top of the boulders of Polar Caves. Thus, New Hampshire can boast of two unique geological rock formations.

Through the following thousands of years, the surface weathered into soil and the primeval forest covered the mountains.

It is doubtful if the Indians discovered Polar Caves, yet they may have secretly used them for hiding their women and children when the Mohawks came on raids. Settlers began to arrive in Rumney after it was granted in 1761.

After the railroad was built in 1850, a hamlet grew at Rumney Depot and another at Rumney Village across the Baker River. These inhabitants were strict Baptists and the Sabbath was a holy day. For amusement the teen-aged youngsters roamed the fields and forest on Sunday.

They discovered a dark opening under a boulder but did not venture within, as they knew that bears and wildcats might have a den there. When young Lloyd French supplied pine knot torches, they explored this cave and discovered that its floor was a sheet of ice. Thus the name was given to Polar Caves.

On future Sabbaths the caves were explored, but this was a profound secret because the youngsters knew this risk to life and limb would be forbidden. After some time the son of Mr. Gallishaw, the village storekeeper, told his father that there was an ice cave down a mile in the valley.

Incredulously Mr. Gallishaw explored and soon the neighborhood was visiting Polar Caves. The principal of the Plymouth Normal School was consulted for advice about exploiting the caves. "Why pour money down those holes" was his reply.

After automobiles began to arrive in increasing numbers, Mr. Gallishaw cleared a parking lot beside Route 25 and erected a cottage for the use of tourists. The teen-aged boys who knew the caves, now older, acted as guides and the fame of Polar Caves became known to the owners of Ausable Chasm, who purchased twenty-nine acres around Polar Caves.

Governor Styles Bridges spoke at a grand opening of the caves and the citizens of Rumney served luncheon to several hundred guests on the Fourth of July, 1936. Today over 50,000 visitors explore the caves annually.

Strong rails along the boardwalks and stairways, and trained guides make the hour trip through the caverns a safe recreation. A cottage contains a lunchroom and one of the most famous gift shops where guests may browse.

Within the park are picnic grounds with a shallow pool where geese and ducks swim and amuse children. A natural rock garden of ferns and lichens covers the boulders and an old sugar house is a museum of ancient farming tools. For students, an unusually complete collection of the minerals that are found in New Hampshire is on display.

Only a few years ago two surprising discoveries appeared in the granite of the boulders. One of the caves is totally dark but when a violet ray was flashed upon its walls, the entire cave glowed with a radioactive effervescence of yellow and green light.

On the ceiling of the corridor to Smuggler's Cave a dripstone of white calcium, about two feet in diameter, has been deposited as moisture has absorbed this element from the granite.

Thus, to young and old, to students and scientists, the

beautiful park at Polar Caves offers pleasure. The location is easily accessible—only four miles from the exit of Highway 93 into Plymouth, with an adequate parking lot beside Route 25.

ALONG THE CONNECTICUT RIVER

Ages ago Mother Nature raised to the surface of New Hampshire several masses of granite peaks. Evans, Pinkham, Crawford, and Franconia notches divide them on the east side of the Connecticut Valley.

On the west side, limestone came to form chains of mountains with Williamstown, Roxbury, and Northfield gulfs between them. Deposits of limestone are in quarries of gray, green, and white marble. It is said the flavor of Vermont maple syrup is derived from the limestone soil.

Flowing between the granite and the limestone is the Connecticut River. Long ago the wide meadows were the beds of shallow lakes that descended like giant steps from the three Connecticut lakes to Long Island Sound.

The history of this valley begins about 1735 around a group of forts called Fort Dummer. Governor Jonathan Belcher established nine "fort towns," named by number, with Chesterfield as Number One and Lempster, Number Nine.

Up the valley Westmoreland was Number Two with a blockhouse to protect a few courageous settlers who had discovered the wide meadows. Number Three became Walpole with Benjamin Bellows the leader. He was an Indian fighter, surveyor, owner of the ferry, and a speculator in land. Bellows Falls, Vermont, was named in his honor.

We suggest packing a hamper for a weekend drive from Hinsdale to Pittsburg along this Connecticut Valley in the foliage season.

At Westmoreland drive up Park Hill to admire the meetinghouse of 1765 with its belfry and Doric columned porch, a remarkable example of the craftsmanship of early woodcarvers in white pine.

The long street at Charlestown, from the two-story homes that now cover the site of Fort Number Four to the present reproduction, preserves the village beauty of the past century.

The river is followed by Route 12A through Claremont to Cornish and the old covered bridge to Windsor, then to Lebanon where we join Route 10 northward.

*Lebanon is a modern city. The Wilder Dam across the Connecticut holds a reservoir that gradually extends to the meadows at Haverhill. Doubtless the town was named from Lebanon, Connecticut, where Moor's Indian School was located before Eleazer Wheelock removed the institution to Hanover and founded Dartmouth College in 1769.

Hanover provides sightseeing at the Hopkins Center with its art galleries and other features; the Baker Library and the old Dartmouth bookstore should be visited.

Ten miles up the valley one looks back 150 years in the beautiful village of Lyme with its 1810 meetinghouse and the horsesheds, the fine colonial homes, and the Alden Tavern, one of the oldest still standing in this country, erected by a descendant of John Alden and Priscilla.

Next Orford claims admiration for its "Ridge"—the old academy building, and far across the green, the Wheeler House designed by architect Charles Bulfinch; the other houses copied from its features.

Rural Piermont leads to Haverhill Corner, with its village green and brick houses, which was cut off from Piermont's boundary to give six miles to Haverhill.

The long Haverhill Street ends in Woodsville with the small island in the river that marks two states and four counties. Cross the Ammonoosuc River into Monroe. Three dams confine the Fifteen Miles Fall: Monroe Dam, Comerford Dam, and in Littleton the Moore Dam which generates the power flowing through the wires all the way into Massachusetts. Another rural town, Dalton, then along wide meadows to Lancaster. The old covered bridge and wide, shaded streets preserve historic tales of the Crawford family.

Northumberland with its old Fort Wentworth and the village of Groveton introduce the lumber industry. The river narrows and the towns of Stratford, Columbia, Colebrook, and Stewartstown are filled with north country atmosphere that recalls Stewart Holbrook's tales of the log drives. Finally, at the end, is Pittsburg and the Connecticut lakes.

The first lake supplies the fisherman with silver salmon and lake trout a yard in length, delicious if the cook is experienced. Nash, Perry, and Indian streams are famous to fishermen also.

Pittsburg was the scene of the Indian Stream Republic. The highways travels on to Quebec.

Drive to the New Hampshire seashore in early summer when the evenings are long over the ocean, to the Lakes Region in midsummer and to the Connecticut Valley in autumn. The return drive on the Vermont side has the landscape of New Hampshire with its White Mountains peaks, attractive villages, and frequent bridges that return the travelers home after a most rewarding adventure.

THE SCHOLAR'S
ALMANACK,
AND FARMER'S
DAILY REGISTER;
FOR THE YEAR OF OUR LORD
1808.

Calculated for the Meridian of Portsmouth, New-Hampshire, latitude 43° 5' N.

SOL. CLARIOR...

By DUDLEY LEAVITT.

GIVE me the ways of wandering stars to know,
The height of Heaven above, and **** below :
Teach me the various labours of the Sun,
And whence proceed the Eclipses of the Moon :
What shakes the solid Earth, what cause delays
The summer night, and shortens winter days ... .vigcrs.

EXETER
Printed by NORRIS & SAWYER. Sold Whole-Sale and Retail at their Book-Store; Sold also by CHARLES PEIRCE, Thomas & Ta an, Portsmouth; and the Booksellers in Boston, Salem, Newburyport, &c. &c.

An early copy of Dudley Leavitt's almanac.

{9}

Of Quakes
and Quakers

WOMEN'S LIB—OLD STYLE

Since the author of the Book of Genesis wrote his story of creation, mankind has accepted the statement that God created man in his own image and that woman was an afterthought. Modern science has disproved the myth yet the status of women is still debatable.

When New Hampshire was settled, rights for women were unknown in the legal sense. They actually possessed nothing. Until a girl married, her father, and after marriage, her husband, held legal control. To the credit of New Hampshire, its public schools have been open to both boys and girls, but its early academies were for boys only. Men were the first public school teachers, in fact, they occupied all professional positions.

Hanging upon the wall of a corridor in the State House at Concord is a portrait of Harriet P. Dame, born in Barnstead in 1815. She was one of the most noted nurses in the Civil War. She volunteered at the beginning of the war when women nurses were forbidden by many generals to enter hospitals in their camps. She was employed in government service for many years and died in 1900.

The insistence of women nurses and the Sanitary Commission established women in professions after the Civil War. The first trained nurse in New England was given her diploma in Boston in 1879.

In colonial days, frequently the family Bible record mentioned that a girl was born on a certain date, often omitted her given name, and her future was forgotten. Girls were often unmentioned in a father's will. Few women owned land, money, houses, or furniture in their homes.

The following copy of a will illustrates the legal status. The will of Ichabod was probated in 1740. "I give and bequeath to my Beloved wife, Rebekah, the following part of my dwelling namely the room next the street, the back chamber, the little pantry room that is parted off the kitchen to be used by her as long as she remains my widow . . . one third part of my homestead land, one third of my orchard, one third of my barn . . . all of my corn, flax, wool and provisions that are by me. Two of my cows, six sheep, a yearling heifer, and one swine, and all of my household goods to be disposed of as she may desire and the right of passing and repassing through the other parts of my homestead land."

The will indicates that a widow did not have the right to her home unless provision was mentioned in her husband's will. Ichabod was unusually generous to his widow. A widow did not possess the goods that she had woven or the spinning wheels and looms.

A mother did not control her own children. Until they were of age the father might place them at work as he wished and collect their wages. In his will he might give his under-age children to anyone he desired or place them under a guardian and the mother could not control this right or any property they might inherit.

In 1903 a bill that provided equal guardianship to parents was introduced into the legislature. Not until 1911 did the men of that body pass such a bill. A husband had the right to punish his wife and children without expecting legal repercussions.

Statistical studies of family genealogies provide revealing reading, especially if ten or more children are recorded. Usually the first wife was the mother of six or seven children. Within three months after her death, a second wife, frequently a widow, accepted the task of rearing the stepchildren and becoming the mother of several offspring of her own. Seldom did she bring into the new marriage the children of her former husband unless she had a small child who needed her care.

When national banks were established, and the earned income of many families was deposited for a checking account, unless a woman possessed her own account, the signature of a married woman was not honored on a bank check.

Gradually housewives became the buyers of the family. Statistics proved that eighty-eight percent of the earned income of a family became the responsibility of the housewife. This required adjustments in policy.

About forty years ago, if the signature of a married woman was registered at a bank, she legally signed checks. Today, the joint account has solved this problem.

The abilities of women find a place in all fields. They are demanding the privilege of an astronaut and they are active in the modern positions of aquanauts.

The evolution of the status of women is a New Hampshire history story of vital importance.

FROM PURITANS TO OSGOODITES

The Toleration Act was a bill passed in the legislature in 1819 that eliminated the "minister's tax" in the towns.

The early town charters contained a provision that the proprietors or their successors must employ a minister and give to him a grant of land. The salary was paid by taxation on property. For this he was to conduct two religious services on the Sabbath Day, assist the families in their legal problems, and teach the children to read the catechism.

The early settlers were Puritans. In 1727 Queen's Chapel was erected in Portsmouth by the Church of England and the Unitarians built the South Church in 1731.

In 1741 an unusually convincing young preacher came to Hampton, named George Whitfield. He declared that everyone should be concerned about his soul; that many people, even ministers and deacons, had lost their faith and were headed for perdition.

The King James version of the Bible was owned in many homes and people began to read it and form their own

ideas about religion. New denominations began to appear.
The first Baptist church was organized in Newton in 1755.
The Scotch-Irish Presbyterians who arrived in 1720 were increasing with thousands of immigrants in the towns of Dublin and Peterborough in the Connecticut Valley.

A leader named John Wesley introduced the Methodist
Discipline. Circuit riders went about on horseback with
their saddle bags filled with literature about their faith.
Meetings were held in kitchens and the religious enthusiasm
of their prayers was heard beyond the walls of the households. The first Methodist church was organized in Chesterfield in 1791. Methodists did not use profane language,
dance, or attend the theater. They discouraged marriage outside of their faith.

Many sects became active. The Quakers who were perse-
cuted in the early years were accepted in Dover and built a
chapel in 1680. Another, built in 1760, is standing today.
Parishes were separated from Portsmouth at Newcastle,
Newington, and Greenland, thus saving miles of walking to
church on the Sabbath. The building at Newington dates
from 1712 where a service of worship has been held every
Sunday since January 1, 1731, by the same parish society.

The Shakers of Enfield and Canterbury, who preferred
not to marry, maintained well-cultivated farms and herds of
fine cattle. Their meetinghouse of 1792 is used today by a
few members of that sect.

The Osgoodites, named for their leader, were active in
the central part of the state many years ago. They looked
for the end of the world about the middle of the nineteenth
century.

Many amusing stories are remembered about these people. They determined the day that the world would end
and refused to plant their fields. Many would have starved
had not their neighbors raised crops for them.

On the appointed day a man watched for the event until
he became so tired that he climbed to the top of a stack of
hay and fell asleep. Some mischievous boys set the hay on
fire. To the amusement of the boys, the sleeper became sud-

denly awake and smelling smoke, exclaimed, "In Hell, just as I expected."

About 1790 taxpayers began to complain because they were paying the ministers' salaries of the early Puritan churches (then called Congregational because this denomination permitted the regular members of the congregation to vote upon parish affairs rather than only the church members).

Bills to change the minister's tax were introduced at the sessions of the legislature but were lost because the majority of the members of the legislature were Congregationalists. Finally in 1819 the old tax was repealed. For a few years many churches continued to demand an annual tax from their members to obtain the salary for the minister.

Thus the religious beliefs developed in New Hampshire in the past three centuries. Many more denominations exist today. These are said to number over two hundred in the United States.

THE NEW ENGLAND STORY
OF DEMON RUM

Looking back through three centuries to the customs of our strict puritanical ancestors, we question with astonishment how the righteous souls became addicted to New England rum.

This story begins when the settlers at Dover began to send their schooners to the Barbados Islands carrying bundles of materials for barrels and hogsheads that were set up there, and filled with sugar and molasses for England. The schooners returned to Dover with supplies for the colony.

Years passed, population increased, shipyards were busy along the banks of the Piscataqua River, and trade was active. The schooners returned from Barbados bringing barrels of rum and distilleries were erected in every hamlet us-

·ing molasses from both the English and French islands of
the West Indies as the main ingredient.

Laws were framed to control the sale of rum and also a
popular beverage that contained rum, called toddy. Among
those who could afford to serve rum, this became the styl-
ish drink to serve to all callers and at social gatherings.

Thus the custom of drinking New England rum became
common. By 1800 everybody used rum freely. When the
counties were established in 1771, licenses were issued to
taverns controlling their permits to sell, and also to retailers.

We quote from the history of a town in the central section of the colony at the beginning of the nineteenth
century: "In 1794 many licenses to mix and sell spiritous liquors for one year were issued. In 1800 New England rum
was the common drink. Grocers kept a barrel for customers, free." When trading day, musters, and bridge raisings were held, the towns furnished the rum.

We know of one North Country community where the
rum drinking got ahead of the church raising. The frame col-
lapsed in a heap along with the workers. It took a second attempt before the framing could be completed.

At ordinations, installations, and church councils, the
churches provided the rum. Ministers served rum to their
callers and everyone treated the minister when he called
upon them. On New Year's Day it was said that the minister
returned to his home finding it difficult to keep his balance.

"It was commendable to get tight." So reads a town
history. A decanter and glasses were placed near the head
of a casket at a funeral for the mourners to take a nip.

The Quakers became alarmed and as early as 1794 made
a rule that a Quaker should not drink. This command was
read at every quarterly meeting and confessions were demanded.

Next the Methodist claimed "that drink was the principal
cause of crime; filled the poorhouses, jails, and state prisons;
made misery in homes; caused rheumatism, gout, and
scrofula; made men brutal; caused early death; and injured
religion, culture, and civilization."

Thinking men began to hold raisings and to cut their hay without rum. At the town meeting, the history states that a law was proposed that no store should sell rum, that only taverns should have the right, but this law was voted down.

About 1850 temperance societies were organized and a pledge of total abstinence was signed by ministers, church members, and alarmed citizens. Doctors encouraged the pledge especially after the Civil War proved that as many soldiers died from drink as from wounds.

The women who had become experienced in the Sanitary Commission during the war organized the Women's Christian Temperance Union in many states. It became national in 1874 with Frances Willard as president. They organized children into "Bands of Hope," and caused the teaching of physiology in the schools with emphasis upon the dangers of drink.

In cities and larger towns saloons where rum was sold night and day lined the streets. Every working man stopped for his drink on the way home from work. Oftentimes he became "ugly drunk" and beat his wife and children before he fell into a stupor.

Men decided that the saloon must be abolished. The Good Templars organization began its work and the eighteenth amendment to the Constitution, prohibiting the manufacture, sale, or transportation of intoxicating liquors, or their importation into the United States, was passed in 1920.

This amendment proved so difficult to enforce that it was repealed on December 5, 1933. Meanwhile saloons disappeared, pure food and drug laws refined injurious elements from many commodities, including intoxicating liquors. New England rum disappeared.

Alcoholics Anonymous societies advertise frequent meetings to combat the dangers of drinking and drugs and the cause of temperance is busy today in New Hampshire.

STATE HOUSES
IN THE GRANITE STATE

New Hampshire became a royal province in 1692 with a governor who was appointed by the king of England and an organized provincial congress or legislature that consisted of representatives from its few organized towns.

The legislature assembled in various towns as more were settled, usually at Exeter or Portsmouth, yet once this assembly, as it was frequently called, met as far north as Charlestown.

Finally in 1758 the legislature voted to build a state house at Portsmouth. This was a wooden building, one hundred feet long and thirty feet wide and two stories in height. Its site was the center of the present Congress Square.

The lower story was an assembly room. The second was divided into three rooms; the first for the king's council, the center for the legislature, and the third belonged to the court of law.

Above the door was a balcony that was used on many occasions. This was the period when Benning Wentworth was governor and revolution was beginning to stir. The hated Stamp Act of 1765 was read from this balcony to a crowd of citizens standing below.

They immediately formed a funeral procession, bearing a coffin that was supposed to contain the body of Liberty. As they approached the intended place of interment, this body showed signs of life. Bells had been tolling, flags were at half staff on the masts of ships on the river, and drums were muffled.

Suddenly cheers sounded, bells began to ring, and the procession returned to the State House in a revolutionary spirit.

One day in March, 1767, again the citizens stood in the square to welcome the arrival from England of John Wentworth, Jr., and to listen to the king's proclamation that appointed him to be the second royal governor of the province.

The crowd escorted Governor Wentworth to his home and the council and other officials entertained him that evening at a banquet, because he was influential in persuading the repeal of the Stamp Act.

Governor Wentworth fled to England when the Declaration of Independence was read from the western steps of the State House on July 18, 1776, to an enthusiastic assembly.

On April 28, 1783, the sheriff of Rockingham proclaimed from the balcony the articles of peace between Great Britain and the colonies.

Again on June 26, 1788, a crowd heard the announcement that the state has ratified the articles of the federal Constitution, becoming the ninth state to do so. This was a day of processions and banquets. On that evening the State House was illuminated with nine lights in each window, probably candles.

The last demonstration was on October 30, 1789, when President George Washington was welcomed by hundreds of troops under General Cilley, with an address by State President John Sullivan, and citizens from the town and surrounding places crowding the entire square.

On that evening a banquet was held and the State House was again illuminated. At the following dance the president met many "beautiful ladies," as noted in the president's diary.

Portsmouth was too far south to remain the capital and the old State House was removed to Court Street in 1836, where a section became a dwelling house. Today this building has been preserved at Strawbery Banke.

During the years of the Revolutionary War the legislature assembled in the more peaceful atmosphere of Exeter but returned to Portsmouth in 1782. At this point, Concord was chosen to become the capital of New Hampshire.

Until 1807, various towns entertained the legislature, but the second meetinghouse in Concord was used for a State House which was situated at the North End on the site of the present county court house.

Additional members crowded this building, and in 1816 the present State House began to be constructed. It was completed in 1819 upon the present site which was presented to the state by the town of Concord.

We are told that at that time no buildings obstructed the view to the banks of the Merrimack River. Who could foretell that within a few years tracks for a railroad would be laid across the meadows.?

The State House was erected at an expense of $82,000. The Senate numbered twelve and the House one hundred ninety members. In 1864 the building was enlarged at a cost of $200,000 and again in 1909 at a cost of $400,000.

The architects copied a design from the Hôtel des Invalides in Paris for this final addition. Today the structure ranks high among other capitol buildings in the United States.

COLONIAL HISTORY IN OLD GARDENS

The Indians taught the settlers to bury a fish in every hill of corn and Mother Nature provided wild grapes, berries, nuts, and wild apple trees. Nobody need starve with deer, bears, wild fowl, and fish in abundant supply.

Sheep and cattle were imported and cuttings from the apple trees of England were grafted upon the native trees that in a few years filled scores of barrels with cider for the winter beverage.

Every family produced something for barter and corn, hay, calves, or lambs were in demand for trading. Sugar and molasses came from the West Indies in exchange for barrel staves.

History relates that homesick women brought bulbs, roots, and seeds from the old flower gardens in England. The offspring of these are flourishing today in New Hampshire. For the best of reasons the lilac was selected for the state flower.

The originator of "Strawbery Banke," Miss Dorothy Vaughn of Portsmouth, is an authority for the statement that the tall lilac shrubs, blooming today beside the Governor Benning Wentworth House erected in 1750 at Little Harbor, are the first lilacs to be brought from England to New Hampshire.

The oldest English pattern garden that is preserved as it was originally planned in 1763, is at the rear of the Moffatt-Ladd House on Daniel Street in Portsmouth. This rises in four terraces from the level of the bank of the Piscataqua River.

The fourth terrace was the vegetable section, the third grew the famous damask rose that still blooms annually. The second contains flower beds where the candium lily bulbs' descendants still thrive. The lower terrace is the lawn with its line of bee hives along one side.

Clinging to the back wall of the three-story house is a wisteria vine. A central path ascends the terraces with turf steps to the upper terrace and fruit trees are scattered in spots to provide shade.

The house is owned by the Society of Colonial Dames of New Hampshire and every feature of the buildings, furniture, and grounds is a cherished heritage from both Portsmouth and old England.

In Epping the original grant to the Burley (Burleigh) family is a remarkable heritage. In its garden are bulbs and plants that are descendants of the early plantings.

On the summit of Blair Hill in Campton, blooming today, is a collection of roses that have been transplanted from abandoned cellar holes along the old range roads in the vicinity of Meredith. When the grant was originally given in 1751, emigrants from England built their block house on the shore of a pond beneath a large white oak tree. The name of the pond today is White Oak Pond. In the garden on the hill bloom the pointed pink buds of the moss rose, the small leaves and blossoms of the native brier rose, and the similar cinnamon rose.

Poplar trees and cinnamon roses bloom today around the

cellar hole of the first home of Samuel Livermore of 1765 in Holderness.

The small, white Scotch rose and the single yellow Huguenonis rose, both with many thorns and tiny leaves, the semidouble red, and the damask white are all in this collection, proving that English emigrants did not forsake their English gardens.

A century ago seed catalogs were not received in the mail. The grocer carried packages of seeds for sweet corn, cabbage, beets, and turnips, but usually the gardener carefully saved a few of his best early peas, dried a few ears of corn, and other varieties, for the next season. Some people still feared to enjoy tomatoes because of poison and the gardener saved his own seeds of a perfect specimen. There were houseplants that housewives proudly displayed. The night blooming cereus aroused widespread curiosity when a neighbor invited her friends on three successive evenings to view one of the ten-inch-wide white blossoms as each opened with a fragrance that was overpowering, as I remember after more than ninety years.

Long vines of English ivy trailed around the living room ceilings and tubs of calla lilies with the large pointed shining leaves and white blossoms with yellow stamens grew in scores of homes, but are seldom seen today.

Lawnmowers were unknown. Some families kept a pet lamb to mow the lawn or the family horse or cow occasionally nibbled the grass. When the first hand lawnmowers appeared, a boy would hurry home from school for the privilege of running the machine. March 4 was the date to plant tomato, cabbage, and celery seeds, to be transplanted in the middle of April and ready for the garden June first. Women planted pansies and "china" asters.

Gardens are real history books.

DUDLEY LEAVITT
AND HIS OLD FARMER'S ALMANAC

Among the names of New Hampshire notables who should be remembered with gratitude is Dudley Leavitt, astronomer, the person who wrote *The Old Farmer's Almanac*. His intellectual capacity was remarkable. This he applied to forecasting weather conditions.

He was born just before the American Revolution in 1772 at Exeter where, in his boyhood, he had the advantages of Phillips Exeter Academy which opened in May, 1783.

He was a descendant of the two earliest governors of Massachusetts: John Winthrop and Thomas Dudley. In 1794 he married Miss Edith Glidden of Gilmanton. They resided the following two years in Gilmanton while Mr. Leavitt studied Greek and Latin at the academy. Later he acquired a knowledge of Hebrew and modern languages.

Dudley Leavitt purchased a large farm in 1806 between Meredith and Center Harbor that remained in the possession of the Leavitt family until recent years. He excelled in mathematics and in his astronomical calculations, interests which occupied him even in his early years.

He published his first *Almanac* in 1797 and continued it until he died in 1851, leaving the calculations for four future years because it was his custom to prepare his data several years in advance of publication. Relatives, the last one named William B. Leavitt, published the *Almanac* after his death.

For a period the *Almanac* passed out of print. Today, thanks to the late Robert Sagendorph, the editor of *Yankee Magazine, The Old Farmer's Almanac* has been revived.

The book contains the same form and information as in its beginning but is greatly enlarged with timely articles on numerous topics.

Next to the Bible and the weekly newspaper the *Almanac* was conspicuous in many homes. It was a book of knowledge. For each month there was a page of daily information. The first column printed the number of the day in the year, then for the month, followed by the time for the rising and the setting of the sun, the time of high and low tide, and the same for the moon.

On the opposite page was the sign of the zodiac, and the position of the sun and the planets, special events on each day such as holidays, the many Saint Days of the church, birthdays of famous persons—and advice to inspect the chimney.

One page advised the day to plant the garden. Corn depended upon the full of the moon. Pictures illustrated the seasons for various tasks as a rail fence in the spring or threshing in the fall. Forecasts for the weather were read daily and believed, although many did not eventuate as predicted.

The United States began its weather bureau observations in 1860. With 10,000 weather stations today they supply correct (more or less) information, but Dudley Leavitt depended upon his mathematical skill and his observations.

In 1811 he began to publish a newspaper, the *New Hampshire Observer,* which he continued several years. He found time to write several books and pamphlets on drawing, the art of music, arithmetic, and a grammar, widely circulated even into Europe.

He was called "Master" Leavitt, as all school teachers were. He taught in District Number Five and later on the Parade Road in Meredith Village. In August, 1819, he opened his Meredith Academic School for young ladies and gentlemen to whom he promised "No pains will be spared to render the acquisition of useful knowledge easy and pleasant."

Board was reasonable. Tuition was $3 per quarter except for the teaching of algebra, navigation, gunnery or the science of projectiles, spheric geometry and trigonometry, astronomy, and philosophy for which the tuition was $3.50 per quarter.

Master Leavitt was noted for his strict discipline, yet his knowledge was such that students attended from far and near. His politeness and reverence for aged persons won great respect.

He had a family of eleven children, of whom nine lived to maturity. One of his sons died immediately previous to his becoming a minister. One daughter married and became a missionary to Siam. Another was a missionary among the Indians in this country.

The old farm was occupied by a granddaughter, Miss Hulda Leavitt and her brother Arthur and his family. His son was Dudley Leavitt, the Weather Man, as he was often called, although he made no special study of the subject. He was well-informed and able to answer questions about astronomy without hesitation.

He was a bachelor and on his death the lakeshore property of the farm was deeded to the town of Meredith for a public park.

Dudley Leavitt, astronomer, sleeps with many of his relatives and descendants in the Leavitt Cemetery on the Quarry Road near the old farm in Meredith.

THE QUAKES GO FAR BACK

A legend in Rye states that an Indian told a settler that one day there was big noise, then the sea came in. The settler may not have realized the meaning of this legend, because the British Isles do not suffer from earthquakes.

Naturally, therefore, the inhabitants of Hampton were frightened when they were aroused from sleep about ten-thirty P.M. on October 25, 1727, by what was to be called "The Great Earthquake."

While the oak frames of their houses shook violently, they did not fall apart, but the chimneys snapped at the roof and the bricks clattered down to the ground.

The weather was clear, no wind was blowing, and soon the noise on the land was answered by the roar of the sea like thunder in the moonlight. Fissures opened in the south part of Hampton and water filled them to form quicksand pools.

The quakes continued during the next two weeks—then two heavy shocks on Christmas Day and occasionally there-after until January 24.

Twenty-eight years later on November 18, 1755, a much more violent shock happened in Hampton about dawn. Again chimneys fell, cattle ran wildly through the fields, and horses reared in their stalls.

This came when the weather was cloudy and rain was falling. The shocks continued in the following two weeks. Finally the town fathers appointed a day of fasting and prayer. The shocks ceased and without doubt, many people believed that their sins were forgiven.

In his diary, Deacon Samuel Lane records seven more earthquakes between 1766 and 1774.

Many persons will recall slight tremors in 1896 and again in 1923 that caused little damage in New Hampshire.

About 2:35 A.M. on December 20, 1940, from the coast northward through Carroll County, an earthquake caused the inhabitants of Rye and of those northern towns to rush into the streets wearing slippers and housecoats, while a roar like thunder filled the air.

Scores of chimneys shattered at the ridgepoles but no buildings fell, although interior damage was widespread and many fragile articles were broken. The cattle lowed in their barns, horses plunged in their stalls, dogs whined and barked, and cats mewed.

Again, at 6:45 A.M. on December 24, 1940, a second shock seemed to be more violent than the earlier quake. Low mutterings were heard during the previous night.

Many peculiar tales were related in the several towns—perhaps the most astonishing was the Wildcat Boulder tale. This large rock, known to hunters because its shape resembled a wildcat, was poised upon the tip of Archer's Ledge about a mile from Route 16 in Ossipee. The morning after the first quake the highwayman was surprised to see this boulder close to the road on the Fernal Dairy Farm.

No trace of a path along the ground that the boulder might have traveled could be found. Probably the force of the earthquake tossed it into the air and it fell down the ledge to the highway.

By careful measurement the water in Ossipee Lake lowered about a foot leaving a vacuum between its surface and the ice that was frozen so solidly it remained unbroken. Many tales were heard that the water completely disappeared—all untrue.

A train filled with skiers left Boston that same day about six A.M. for Conway. As the train approached Newton Junction, the engine began to shake back and forth.

As the engineer shut the throttle, he shouted, "What in Tophet ails her?" Coal and water were falling from the tender. After safely arriving at Dover, and the trouble was discovered, a careful test was made of the engine and slow time followed to Conway, for along the track for miles a crack about a foot wide was noted.

Another event was the sudden striking—at least 130 strokes—of the clock on the library at Conway, a real surprise because the clock had been silent for many years. The clock awoke for seventy more strokes the next day.

A fire from a cracked chimney caused $5,000 damage in Tamworth and another in Conway for $300. At poultry 250 turkey eggs and 1500 chicken eggs never hatched. Heavy cream churned to butter and telephone poles were tossed up, but their wires held them upright.

The famous Sheriff James Welch of Tamworth exclaimed, "Well! I'll be!" when he watched two chimneys fall, a Christmas tree shed its needles, and a water pipe spray his head when the pipe broke.

Apparently an underground fault extends inland along the Continental Shelf and northward along the Saco Valley, since these disturbances center in this section of New Hampshire.

Geologists say that when the silt from the land upsets the balance of the bed of the sea along the coast an earthquake occurs.

SUPERSTITIONS OF YESTERYEAR

In these days of scientific knowledge, it is difficult to comprehend the mental suffering that our ancestors endured because of their fear of the devil and other evil spirits. Many old wives tales about ghosts, witches, and dreams are not yet forgotten.

The Puritans believed in "signs of the times" such as an eclipse of the sun, a sudden earthquake, or the appearance of a comet which caused them to appoint a day of fasting and prayer to seek pardon for their sins.

Scores of colonial homes were supposed to be haunted by ghosts. The most famous were the Moulton residence in Hampton and the Ocean Born Mary house in Henniker.

Men carried a lucky coin in a pocket. If a right hand itched, one should wet his finger in his mouth and rub the spot with it. Money would certainly be found.

If a garment were donned wrong side out, never change it to the right side or the day would be unlucky.

My practical mother remarked one day, "Better be cautious today, I saw the new moon over my left shoulder last evening." Evidently the warning that her grandmother taught to her was remembered.

While riding with father, suddenly he tightened the reins to hasten the horse, preventing a squirrel from crossing the road ahead of us. "Of course I am foolish," said father. "I somehow like to stop a squirrel. They used to say we might have an accident."

When an old mirror fell into many pieces because the old, red cord happened to break my hostess said, "You do not seem to be worried." I asked, "Should I?" She replied, "Certainly! This is a warning that you will suffer a serious illness." The warning failed to bring trouble.

The Bible states in the old Hebrew law, "Never allow a witch to live." The Puritans in Massachusetts obeyed this law by hanging several "witches." In many towns in New Hampshire women were accused of witchcraft, but none were convicted of the crime although Goody Cole was cruelly abused in Hampton.

A typical story about a witch was told by a reliable old woman in Plymouth. One of the oldest houses remaining in the village today was the residence of the village doctor who owned a valuable horse that his teenage son was permitted to ride occasionally.

In the late afternoon the doctor was called to visit a patient at some distance from his home. The lad decided that this was a favorable opportunity for a ride up the valley.

After traveling quietly more than a mile, the horse suddenly became almost unmanageable. Only after beating the animal severely about the head was he able to turn about toward home.

Although he attempted to remove the results of the whipping, traces were visible. Dismayed by expectations of his father's anger, the boy passed a restless night. Toward morning he crept quietly to the stable. To his astonishment, no marks of the beating remained. Thankfully he returned to his bed.

On the way to school in the morning he learned that Granny Ober who lived up the valley was unable to leave her bed because of a severe beating that she had suffered the evening before. The boy decided that the aged witch had caused his horse to become unruly.

In Peterborough hot water was dashed upon the back of a vicious black cat. Apparently the cat suffered no harm, but a well-known witch was said to have been seriously burned on her back.

When the cream in the churn did not turn to butter after hours of using the dasher, boiling hot water poured into the churn would soon bring the cream to butter. A witch was always blamed for the long delay.

The Scotch-Irish in Derryfield believed that a fairy named Neto was constantly assisting people in trouble. They claimed that Neto caused the Indians who had captured Hannah Dustin and the boy prisoner to sleep while they were killed. Then Neto guided Hannah and boy safely back to their homes in Haverhill. It was claimed that John Stark, a Scotch-Irishman, led a charmed life. The fairies did not permit bullets to harm him.

A strange custom was followed in some villages when a death occurred in a family that owned bees. A member of the family went among the hives to tell the bees about the loss to prevent them from leaving the hives.

Experts now discuss mental health, psychoanalysis, and ecology. People worry no longer about ghosts and evil spirits nor fear the cloud-capped summits as did the Indians.

With the wonder of TV and radio, men have been watched as they walk upon the moon and their voices are heard from a distance of 225,000 miles in space.

We read the Russians cultivated cabbages in a spaceship.

But has science banished superstition?

GRANITE STATE FAIRS

As is well known, the custom of managing fairs has been practiced in Europe for many centuries with competition for prizes for exhibits and races. This custom was introduced into New Hampshire by the Scotch-Irish after they settled in Nutfield (now Londonderry) in 1719.

In 1722 Governor Shute granted to Nutfield the right to an open market and two fairs, one on May 8, the other on October 8 unless those dates were on the Sabbath. If so, then on the following Monday. The October fair proved popular for about a century.

Other fairs were advertised in the *Portsmouth Gazette* in 1779, one at the home of Abraham Libby in Rye, the other in the house of Enoch Coffin in Epping.

Within the charters that Governor Benning Wentworth granted to towns, permission is found that when the town contained fifty families, an open market might be held and two fairs on certain days of the year.

County agricultural societies began to be organized in 1814 for the purpose of improving agriculture and for "domestic manufacturing" meaning spinning and weaving that was produced in the homes.

In 1817 the legislature granted state aid in varying amounts from $100 to $500 to Coos County if a fair was sponsored in that northern county. Then in 1820 reports of how the aid was used were demanded before this money was paid to the counties.

Seven years later all money from the state was withdrawn because the farmers did not care about fairs and were too stubborn to offer exhibits.

One legislator said that he disapproved of driving oxen thirty miles and compelling them to drag heavy loads for money and to permit men to wager on this cruelty. He considered this promoted cruelty, immorality, and dissipation.

Transportation was a hindrance in 1824, especially for farmers who were not within a radius of ten miles of a fair. One hundred years earlier, the Scotch-Irish were growing potatoes and weaving linen to barter with their neighbors in Salem which was their reason for their fairs.

Twenty-five years later a group of enthusiastic leaders organized the State Agricultural Society with Franklin Pierce as president. He was soon to be elected the president of the United States.

This society promoted expansive fairs for ten or more years. The sites were selected by bids and four were won by Manchester. Racing by horses was the drawing event. Trains brought crowds from all parts of the state.

Their final fair was at Manchester in 1860. Rain prevented the last grand race until the morning after the fair closed.

In 1870 the Commission of Agriculture was revived by the legislature and small subsidies were occasionally provided for fairs and off and on county and town fairs were promoted.

Next the Grange became powerful and Tilton was the center of their activities. Trains were filled with attendants at their fairs.

Finally in 1928 the Commissioner of Agriculture, Andrew L. Felker, organized the State Fair Association with efficient officers. The state veterinarian, Dr. Robinson W. Smith was secretary and treasurer for many years. Fairs have flourished ever since.

Since 1939 eight fairs have paid over $500 in premiums and shared a $3,500 legislative subsidy. The Rochester Fair has been longest in existence with the Plymouth Fair second under several organizations.

At present the fairs are assisted by a bonus of one quarter of one percent of the pari-mutuel wagers of the Rockingham Race Track. This is used for premiums.

Today, to attend a fair is an education in agriculture; 4-H clubs and the New Hampshire Arts and Crafts exhibit culinary skills, needle crafts, and vegetables and flowers.

The final fair of the year is the famous Sandwich Fair on Columbus Day, October 12. Thousands of people regard this event as the closing feature of the fall season. Autumn usually scatters its colors, the tourist day is done.

To appreciate the skills that are practiced in New Hampshire, we advise attending its fairs.

(Many of the facts in this story were derived from an article written by the State Historian, Leon W. Anderson, with the title "New Hampshire Fairs—1722-1870.")

MARY'S LITTLE LAMB
BECOMES LEGEND

Since I am ninety-five years young, it may not be amiss to include a bit of reminiscence now and then. One of my childhood habits was to constantly be singing. Ninety-three years ago grandmother taught me the words of "Mary had a little lamb."

Some of the older readers may recall the three stanzas that related how Mary's lamb followed her to school and was turned outside the school house, yet still it lingered near.

About fifty years ago Henry Ford purchased the Mary Lamb Schoolhouse at Sterling, Massachusetts, and removed it to Sudbury, Massachusetts, where he was interested in restoring the Wayside Inn.

Mrs. Sarah Josepha Hale, publisher of *Godey's Magazine*, published the original poem and her own additional stanzas in 1830. The original Mary's married name was Tyler. She was born in 1806 and died in 1889.

Soon after, I learned that a second Mary's Schoolhouse was in Newport, New Hampshire, where the supposed author of the poem taught a school either before her marriage or after she became a widow.

The name of Sarah Josepha Hale had been familiar to me when in my girlhood my mother was a subscriber to *Godey's Magazine* which Mrs. Hale edited—a popular fashion monthly that made her name a household word.

The illustrated designs of elegant gowns, in color, with their wide skirts spread over hoops often six or more feet in diameter at their hems, with trimmings of fringe and lace, became collectors' items. The monthly arrival of *Godey's* was anticipated eighty years ago for it published the latest fashions, recipes,household hints, and a romantic story.

About 1925, among my friends was Miss Mary Sawyer of Providence, Rhode Island, the state president of the Federation of Women's Clubs.

Miss Sawyer was indignant to learn that Newport, New Hampshire, was claiming that Mrs. Hale was the author of the Mary's lamb poem. Miss Sawyer was a direct descendant and namesake of the original Mary Sawyer who owned the lamb.

Miss Sawyer was able to show proof of her claim by displaying a copy of the *National Magazine* of 1870 that had printed the three stanzas of the poem with the name of its author, John Roulestone of Sterling, Massachusetts.

Miss Sawyer's story was that a ewe sheep disowned her offspring, as frequently occurs. Little Mary was assigned the task of feeding the baby lamb by soaking a cloth in milk for the lamb to suck, until she taught it to lap milk from a dish.

The lamb became the constant companion of Mary and managed to follow her to school one day. This so pleased the children but the teacher turned the lamb outside the schoolhouse. The lamb stayed about until Mary appeared.

Young John Roulestone happened to visit the school on that day. He was so amused at the incident that he composed the poem. It became popular when it was published in a collection of Mother Goose rhymes and was given a tune that children in my childhood learned to sing.